ALSO BY JENNIFER ARNOLD

"Transformative . . . A perfect balance of science and observation, this book . . . is a worthy to our canine friends." —*Publishers Weekly*

"Charming." —*The Washington Post*

"Arnold's voice is assertive with experience.... Her storehouse of anecdotal evidence is telling and entertaining, and her demolition of various alpha-model and negative reinforcement teaching techniques is thorough and lofty." —*Kirkus Reviews*

In a Dog's Heart

In a Dog's Heart

A COMPASSIONATE GUIDE
TO CANINE CARE, FROM ADOPTING
TO TEACHING TO BONDING

JENNIFER ARNOLD

SPIEGEL & GRAU

2013 Spiegel & Grau Trade Paperback Edition

Copyright © 2011 by Jennifer Arnold

Published in the United States by Spiegel & Grau,
an imprint of The Random House Publishing Group,
a division of Random House, Inc., New York.

SPIEGEL & GRAU and Design is a registered trademark of
Random House, Inc.

Originally published in hardcover in the United States by Spiegel & Grau,
an imprint of The Random House Publishing Group,
a division of Random House, Inc., in 2011.

Photos courtesy of David C. Scott appear on pages iv, xiv,
2, 52, 58, 94, 154, 168, 188, 202, 210, 214, 228
Photos courtesy of Del Monte Foods appear on pages 8, 74, 108, 218
Photos courtesy of Chris Casatelli appear on pages 16, 34,
124, 134, 146, 178, 186, 198, 222

Library of Congress Cataloging-in-Publication Data

Arnold, Jennifer
In a dog's heart : a compassionate guide to canine care, from adopting
to teaching to bonding / Jennifer Arnold.
p.   cm.
ISBN 978-0-8129-8245-9
eBook ISBN 978-0-679-64372-2
1. Dogs—Psychology.   2. Dogs—Behavior.
3. Human–animal relationships.   I. Title.
SF422.86.A756 2011
636.7—dc23   2011023596

Printed in the United States of America

www.spiegelandgrau.com

2 3 4 5 6 7 8 9

Book design by Susan Turner

For Neil and Margaret, now and always

and

For Chase, who teaches me about dogs every day

Dogs have given us their absolute all. We are the center of their universe. We are the focus of their love and faith and trust. They serve us in return for scraps. It is without a doubt the best deal man has ever made.

—Roger Caras

CONTENTS

In a Dog's Heart

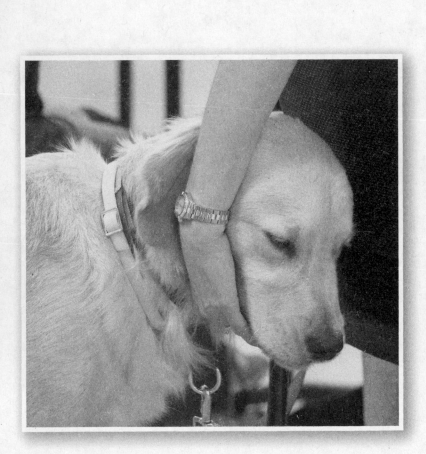

In Their Heart of Hearts

I'd first noticed the anxious mother when my dog Butch and I arrived at our departure gate at the massive Hartsfield-Jackson Atlanta International Airport. She was near the boarding area, jiggling a crying baby and holding the hand of a beautiful little girl who appeared to be about three years old. Looking at the sea of people crowded around the entrance to the jetway, I decided to give Butch a drink of water and a few treats before attempting to board the plane. After filling his bowl, I glanced back at the young mother. She was trying to get the busy gate agent's attention, undoubtedly to ask if she and her children could preboard to get settled, but the crowd was blocking her from his view. The baby was now quiet, still in her mother's arms, but I could no longer see the little girl. Just at that moment, Butch pulled away from me, weaving through the sea of legs surrounding the boarding area. I scrambled along in his wake.

When I finally caught up, I found him nuzzling the little girl who'd gone missing. The mom and I had reached the pair simultaneously, and upon seeing her mother, the child pitifully wailed, "Mommy, I got lost but this saver dog came to help me." Then she wrapped her arms around Butch's neck and started crying. After a few deep sobs, she snuffled out a little giggle and said, "He has a really big head." As the mom watched Butch tenderly snuggle with her little girl, a look of understanding came over her face. In that instant, she recognized the profound impact Butch was having on her daughter. In a very quiet and serious tone, she said, "I suspect this dog has an even bigger heart."

She was absolutely correct. Butch has a huge heart. I was fortunate enough to tour for my first book, *Through a Dog's Eyes,* with Butch beside me every step of the way. He might be the kindest, most patient creature I have ever known. He graciously greeted hundreds of people, even though there were times when he was so tired he'd fall asleep standing up, between greetings. Bigger than all of Texas is my Butch's heart. But then, I suspect that most dogs have big hearts.

After the airport incident, I couldn't stop thinking about the heart of a dog. Not the actual heart that pumps blood, but the metaphoric heart: the very essence of the individual. I thought about the fact that my mom used the expression *in my heart of hearts* when she wanted to convey her seriousness about a particular matter. I was amazed when, at my very next book signing, a lovely older woman asked me, "What do you think dogs really want, in their heart of hearts?" Before I could tell her that I'd been thinking about that for days, her husband asked, "And why should I pay for it?" We all laughed, but the more I thought about it, the more I recognized that these were valid questions.

What do dogs want and need in their heart of hearts, and why does it behoove us to give it to them? My short answer to the woman's question is, "Dogs simply want to be happy, and they want us to be happy with them." My answer to her husband's question is, "Their value to our world far exceeds whatever they might cost us!"

CHAPTER ONE

What Dogs Want

"He's just a baby," the woman told me. "But he seems so with-drawn." A rescue group had taken in the mixed-breed dog and re-quested that I evaluate his potential for rehabilitation and rehoming. The dog, Otter, had gotten himself into trouble by growling at the people who owned him. As Otter climbed out of a big SUV, I could see that he was young, and despite the fact that he was wearing a basket muzzle, he hardly looked aggressive. His paws and head were entirely too big for his bony body, and he seemed to have difficulty coordinating all four of his lanky legs. However, when I looked into his eyes, any resemblance to a puppy quickly disappeared. They belonged to a much older soul, one that was not so much angry as it was weary.

I knelt sideways in front of Otter, my gaze averted, allowing him to determine whether it was safe to approach me. We stayed motion-less for several long minutes. Finally, he took two small steps toward me, lowering his head, resigned to whatever fate awaited him. I did not want Otter to approach in fear, so I slowly inched away.

"Maybe we can get Otter to follow another dog into the building," I suggested to the woman holding the puppy's long leash. I knew from the rescue group's intake form that his owners, an older couple, had used a trainer to help teach Otter his house manners. The trainer had advised the couple to squirt hot sauce in the dog's face when he jumped up to greet them. She also provided a remote shock collar, to be used when he did something they considered inappropriate. So it was clear that Otter was scared to death of people. As we stood in the driveway at Canine Assistants, the nonprofit I founded that provides service dogs to people with disabilities, I knew the only comfort I could offer him was the companionship of another dog.

A pretty female golden retriever quickly worked her magic on Otter. He followed her into our office, where he allowed me to unclip his muzzle and leash. The woman from the rescue program said her goodbyes and, without thinking, reached to give Otter a pat. The dog suddenly shied away, as if her hand were a hot iron.

"What on earth will you do with this poor dog?" the woman asked me, as she turned to leave.

"We'll start by getting him healthy and showing him that he is now safe. If we can, we will earn his trust and teach him some skills so he can gain a little confidence. As one of my friends says, we have to earn the right to be heard."

"That poor dog deserves a good life," the woman said. "I hope you can give it to him."

In 1943, Abraham Maslow, a psychology professor at Brandeis University, published a paper titled "A Theory of Human Motivation," in which he proposed a construct of human needs. Human needs, he believed, evolve sequentially from the most basic to the more advanced, forming a pyramid that culminates in a self-actualized individual when the needs at each successive level have been met. Since its publication, Maslow's hierarchy of needs, as his theory is known, has come under some criticism as, among other things, ethnocentric and exceedingly individualistic. This criticism aside, Maslow's hierarchy provides an excellent basis for describing the needs of dogs and how they rank and structure their most valued necessities. To better describe dogs' needs, I have adapted Maslow's work for my own use and named the pyramid Canine Construction, or C2 for short.

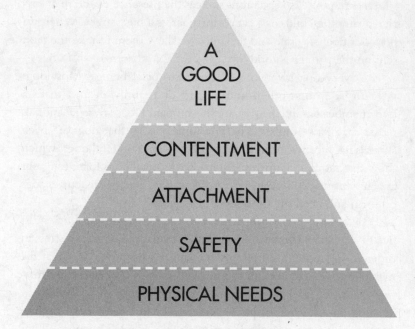

A
GOOD
LIFE

CONTENTMENT

ATTACHMENT

SAFETY

PHYSICAL NEEDS

The principles are relatively simple. Initially, all efforts will (and must) be directed to meet the base requirement of canine existence, the first level: *physical needs*. A dog's primary instincts demand that if he is hungry or thirsty, he focus all of his energy on obtaining food and water. Subsequently, if he has no immediate shelter, the dog must concentrate on finding a way to keep his body temperature regulated. Likewise, if he is sick, his illness becomes his singular concern. Fundamentally, a dog must have a healthy body. Only after that has been addressed can the dog turn his full attention toward the next level: *safety*.

This second level of the pyramid is of critical importance in the life of any living being, and certainly dogs are no different. Our dogs have no way of understanding that the yard is safe but the street is dangerous. Nor do they understand that something isn't safe to swallow simply because they can fit it into their mouths. Dogs, like toddlers, must be protected from the dangers lurking in the outside world. Sometimes they must be protected from even their own instinctive responses to situations such as the presence of the mail carrier, a running child, or a cat dashing across a busy street. When we help our dogs stay safe and feel safe, we allow them to take the next step on the path to a good life.

As every dog lover knows, dogs are social beings. Most dogs want to be around others and be part of a family, even if that's a two-member family: the dog and his human. Dogs are *social* animals rather than *pack* animals. The prevailing theory that dogs are pack animals has recently been challenged by studies on feral dogs, which show that rather than forming stable packs, feral dogs form transient attachments to one another. Regardless of its specific structure, dogs do form and need the third level: *attachment*.

Contentment is the fourth level in the C2 pyramid. Dogs must live in predictable environments with a manageable level of stress in order to be content. Although occasional adventures are great for maintaining excitement in a dog's life, most dogs crave daily routine. And, whether it is assisting someone who uses a wheelchair, keeping the yard free of pesky squirrels, or just being your faithful companion, every dog needs a raison d'être. Having purpose allows dogs to develop self-confidence and garner the respect of those around them, important components in the life of a content dog.

Understanding what our dogs need is relatively simple; determining our role in meeting those needs is considerably more complex. This book addresses how to help your dog successfully negotiate the progressive levels of the C2 pyramid. It discusses the practical issues involved in meeting his physical needs, such as veterinary care, first aid, feeding schedules, and exercise protocols. It details how to keep him safe from both extrinsic dangers, such as becoming lost, and intrinsic dangers, such as biting. It outlines how to choose the right dog for your lifestyle and, by so doing, help him be successful and content.

This book was written because I love dogs. But I also believe in dogs, and I believe that when we are presented with the opportunity to have a relationship, based in mutual trust and understanding, with a dog, we are being offered a gift—one that offers both species myriad rewards. Throughout the book are stories of the extraordinary ways in which dogs prove themselves worthy of our care and devotion, and how we can, and why we should, help them achieve what they so deserve—*a good life.*

CHAPTER TWO

The Gift of Good Health

Amber is a beautiful, small golden retriever, placed with a little boy named Jack who has Duchenne muscular dystrophy. Although Amber had clearly given her heart to Jack, she adored the entire family. She responded to each member that came in with polite, if reserved, warmth. Jack's mom was perhaps most impressed by Amber's apparent recognition that Jack's grandmother, an almost daily visitor to their house, was older and somewhat fragile. For the first several months after the placement, Amber was quietly cautious around the grandmother, acknowledging her presence but keeping a distance. So it was a shock to everyone when one day the elderly woman walked into the house and Amber began frantically jumping all over her and whining loudly. Nothing seemed to appease Amber. Day after day the behavior continued when the grandmother entered the house: Amber would not be still.

Several months after the behavior started, Jack's grandmother had a regular checkup that revealed she was suffering from lymphoma. She began treatment immediately. Amber stopped jumping and crying as suddenly as she had started the odd behavior. When I asked Jack's mom if she believed Amber realized the grandmother was gravely ill, she said, "Don't you see? She knew it long before we did. Once it was clear we understood, she no longer had to try and tell us something was wrong."

Although this is a remarkable story, in my experience and in the accounts of animal behaviorists and dog owners alike, it is far from rare. Cancer researcher Michael McCulloch says, "The dog's brain and nose hardware is currently the most sophisticated odor detection device on the planet." As a matter of fact, McCulloch's work at the Pine Street Foundation has led him to conclude that it is possible for dogs to be trained to detect lung and breast cancer from the exhalations of human patients. It is widely believed that cancer cells produce a metabolic waste that differs from the waste produced by healthy cells. McCulloch contends that this unique chemical signature in the patient's breath is detectable by dogs. Other researchers have further concluded that dogs can be taught to distinguish slight differences in these chemical signatures, helping determine which type of cancer is present. The presence of skin, ovarian, bladder, bowel, and kidney cancers may be sensed by a dog's nose even before they are detectable through other forms of testing.

Several years ago, I was in a large grocery store just outside of Dallas for a Milk-Bone presentation. I had Butch, my goldendoodle and Canine Assistants spokesdog, with me. After the presentation, Butch and I were aimlessly drifting down the pet aisle when a woman spotted us. She looked at me briefly and then down at Butch, staring at him for so long and with such intensity it seemed as if she were counting each of his wavy hairs. She noticed me watching her and looked away quickly but then turned back again. She slowly walked over to us. "You may not believe this"—she paused—"but a dog just like this one probably saved my husband's life."

She and her husband, Tom, had a three-year-old goldendoodle named Rufus. One day Tom was lying on the floor playing with Rufus, throwing a chew toy and wrestling for control. Suddenly the dog stood over Tom, sniffing and lightly nibbling the man's lower lip. Her husband assumed it was part of the game Rufus was playing and lay there quietly, until he realized that Rufus was attempting to bite a sore just on the inside of Tom's mouth. Before Tom could move Rufus away, the big dog bit down on the sore hard enough to make it bleed. Tom knew that Rufus wasn't being aggressive, but he couldn't understand why Rufus would bite the inside of his mouth, or why Rufus didn't seem to want to leave him alone even as Tom pushed him away.

Tom could not stop the bleeding inside his mouth after more than an hour of trying, and he ended up in the emergency room of a nearby hospital. The physician saw the bleeding sore and immediately called an oral surgeon. What Tom thought was a canker sore was actually oral cancer. The spot was surgically removed the following morning; the cancer had not spread. The woman believed that without Rufus, her husband would have ignored the sore until it might have been too late for him to receive successful treatment.

It isn't just cancer that dogs appear able to detect. They seem to know, and care, about a number of things that can go wrong in the human body.

One evening, a very tired Kay was walking through her college cafeteria with her seizure-response dog, Greer. She had just gotten off work and wanted nothing more than to crawl into her bed for a good night's sleep. Greer had other ideas.

Normally very good at walking right beside Kay, Greer began to pull hard on her leash. Nothing Kay did calmed her normally placid dog. Kay became irritated with Greer. "I'm too tired for this. Get a grip," she admonished the golden. After rounding a corner, Kay saw what was so upsetting to Greer. Two girls were slowly lowering a third to the floor as she began having a seizure. Greer ran to the girl on the ground and snuggled next to her—just as she does when Kay has a seizure. The school nurse on duty was notified and quickly arrived to care for the girl.

The nurse proclaimed that the girl was coming out of the seizure just as Greer moved from next to the girl to on top of her. Greer began whining and looking pleadingly at Kay. "Something's not right," Kay told the nurse. "Everything's fine. She's just recovering," the nurse replied. "Get that dog off of her." Greer would not be moved and continued to whine. By then, Kay was carefully watching the girl. "She isn't breathing!" Kay shouted to the nurse.

The young girl had gone into cardiac arrest. Undoubtedly the timing coincided with Greer's whining and change of position. As Greer watched, the girl was successfully resuscitated.

"She knew," Kay told me several days later. "She didn't care how upset I got with her. She knew that girl, a total stranger, needed her."

On January 4, 2011, *The New York Times* ran an editorial by Hal Herzog, author and professor of psychology at Western Carolina University, that focused on the lack of well-validated evidence that pets positively affect human health. Susan, my literary agent, was incensed by the tone of the piece. It intimated that many people, such as veterinarian and author Marty Becker, were bamboozling the public into believing that pets are good for us, and it questioned whether or not pets are worth the money they cost. He did all this under the guise of calling for better studies on the human-animal bond. Susan suggested I write a rebuttal. I declined, never wanting to appear to be discouraging of more scientific research.

I was wrong not to respond. Common sense tells us that our dogs are good for us, and it is precisely because of the failure of people such as Herzog to credit this common sense that dogs have been devalued and underestimated by many in society. Without a doubt, dogs—indeed, all companion animals—positively affect the physical health of the humans who love them. Repeated studies have indicated that pets lower blood pressure, while others have shown that interacting with dogs floods us with soothing hormones such as oxytocin. Whether or not the studies were scientifically well designed is largely irrelevant to me as a dog lover. I know they get us out of bed each day, forcing us to move, bend, and stretch, if only in our efforts to care for them. The anecdotal evidence in support of the theory that dogs positively impact our health is far more compelling than any to the contrary. The effect a dog has on a human life can be nothing short of miraculous.

A little boy I know named Tyler was born at twenty-nine weeks' gestation, weighing a scant two pounds. He was missing chromosome 7, a birth defect that often has fatal consequences. Tyler is now six years old, and although he has spent much of his young life in the hospital, he continues to fight hard to survive.

When he was five, during one of his many hospitalizations Tyler went to a very special party, held in the children's hospital to celebrate the birthday of one of the hospital staffers, a Canine Assistants facility dog named Casper. The big dog was turning two, and many patients, doctors, and hospital workers came to celebrate their unique staff member's birthday. Tyler wouldn't have missed the party. He and Casper had a special connection from the moment they met. They were best friends.

Tyler tolerates going to the hospital because he knows Casper will be there. As soon as the little boy gets settled in his room, the nurses know to call down and request a visit from the staff dog. When asked what he wants to be when he grows up, Tyler replies, "The doctor who gets to take Casper around to make the kids all better."

Tyler's most recent hospitalization had been an extremely difficult one. The little boy's body seemed as if it had given up. He lost consciousness, and soon after that he lost the ability to breathe on his own. He was placed on a ventilator. His pupils became fixed and dilated. His family was told that this was almost certainly the end for the little boy. It was unlikely that he would recover.

Extended family and friends were notified of Tyler's condition, among them Casper's owner, a full-time employee at the hospital. Not long after, Casper ran into the boy's hospital room. His usual bouncy, happy demeanor disappeared in an instant as he noticed the child lying motionless. Ever so slowly and gently, the large dog lifted himself onto the little boy's bed. Once there, Casper lay down next to the boy, put his head on his paws, and silently stared at Tyler with unwavering intensity. For long minutes, Casper did not move. Finally, the dog reached out a paw to gently touch Tyler; then, scooting himself up, he softly licked the boy's small hand. Tyler's mother, sitting on the other side of the bed, thought she felt the little boy move his shoulder, but she dismissed that as wishful thinking, a result of the ventilator vibration. Casper licked Tyler's hand again and pressed himself against the boy. This time, there was no mistaking the deliberate movement the child made as he wiggled his fingers in response to the dog's touch.

Family and medical personnel watched in amazement as Tyler slowly returned to consciousness. The boy's grandmother told me, "It was as if Casper willed our boy back." Once Tyler's eyes opened, Casper's silent vigil was over. The big dog rolled over on his side, stretched, let out a sigh, and began wagging his tail.

The doctors do not dismiss Casper's contribution to Tyler's recovery. "A patient's will to live can make the difference in these situations," one of Tyler's medical team explained. "Maybe it was Casper's touch that influenced that will."

Dogs permeate our lives. We are linked as species, a link solidified by thousands of years of living together. The laws of nature state that if the relationship were detrimental to either species it would not have endured. We are continually finding new ways in which humans and dogs can and do benefit one another.

Casper is a golden retriever mix trained by Canine Assistants. He works full-time at a children's hospital: Children's at Scottish Rite in Atlanta. His daily routine consists of visiting children in their rooms, going to the oncology department while chemotherapy is being given, and lending encouragement in the physical rehabilitation center. When Casper is with the kids, they lie quietly while medication drips through their IVs or bravely remain still as the MRI machine pounds loudly. Every day the kids ask their nurse when Casper will come to visit.

One day, Lisa, the Scottish Rite volunteer coordinator with whom Casper lives, was on her way out of the hospital when a call came from the fourth-floor nurses' station. A nurse said, "Dr. Davis needs Casper for a consultation." Lisa responded that she was late for a meeting. "Just give me the name of Dr. Davis's patient and the room number and Casper will come for a visit as soon as we get back," she responded. There was a long pause on the other end. "I don't think you understand," the nurse said. "*Dr. Davis* needs a few minutes with Casper . . . she's had a very rough morning."

The value of an animal who can reduce stress and uplift mood shouldn't be underestimated.

While Casper's job is to buoy spirits, Lisa's job is to keep Casper healthy. Lisa believes in feeding Casper only the highest-quality food, providing plenty of clean water, and seeing that he gets ample exercise and excellent healthcare. Although Casper has been hailed as a hero for his work at the hospital, all dogs deserve Casper's way of life. Unfortunately, not all dogs get what they deserve.

CHAPTER THREE

Keeping Our Dogs Healthy

Crazy people are not new to me. I'm a Southern woman, culturally conditioned to appreciate eccentricity; nonetheless, I often find myself stunned by the depravity of some people who profess to love animals.

Several months ago I spoke with a woman, Lana, who had just adopted a four-year-old male German shepherd, Spritz, from a rescue group. Lana explained that she was at her wits' end with the dog. She had paid for an expensive online training course but still couldn't get the dog to pay any attention to her. "It's like he can't even see me," she said in desperation. With my curiosity aroused by her description, I made an appointment to see Lana and Spritz the following weekend.

Their house was located in a gated community, and I was pleased to see that an acre of their yard was fenced, giving Spritz a nice area in which to romp. Unfortunately, my positive observations ended there.

When I first met Spritz, I noticed that he was severely underweight, and despite having a five-foot-high fence surrounding him, he was chained to a tree. Most dogs who are chained will bark and fuss when approached by a stranger. As I moved close, Spritz shuffled to his feet. He didn't bark or wag his tail or even cower; he just stood lethargically in place.

Lana came out and immediately told me that she had done everything she had learned online to prepare Spritz for my visit. Spritz had not been fed for thirty-six hours and had been chained without water for the past eight. In response to my horrified expression, she told me that the online trainer said dogs learned best when they were very thirsty, hungry, and deprived of the ability to move freely or make social contact. I was shocked. Lana had actually paid someone a good deal of money to tell her how to torture her dog—a dog who had been a stray just two months earlier.

I explained to Lana as calmly as possible that the theories behind those deprivation strategies have been around for many years, and that on a very limited basis, used by someone who knows what they are doing, they can be somewhat useful. For example, when you use a dog's breakfast kibble as training treats, the dog's hunger works in your favor. Likewise, if you have been away from your dog for a brief time, his excitement in seeing you might help him focus. The problem is that techniques such as this can easily morph into cruelty. And no living being learns well when his survival needs are not being met. Remember the pyramid of needs: If you are truly hungry, you become fixated on finding food. If you are dehydrated, getting water is your main priority, not learning to sit on cue. Lana was shaken by my explanation and promised not to continue using the techniques she had leaned from her online trainer.

Spritz was going to need several weeks of good food and TLC before we could teach him any behaviors. Lana readily agreed to allow a friend of mine, a lover of shepherds, to take Spritz home with her for a while. Six weeks later, I drove Spritz back to Lana's house. He was still slender, but sleek rather than gaunt, his coat and eyes shining with good health. Lana couldn't believe he was the same dog. I demonstrated the behaviors that my friend had taught Spritz to perform on cue, such as *sit, down, freeze, high-five,* and *take a bow.* As we worked, Spritz never took his eyes off my face, and his tail never stopped wagging.

I see Spritz every few weeks. He continues to gain weight and learn new tricks. Lana is now actively involved in explaining to other dog owners how important it is to assure dogs, especially rescues, that their survival needs will be met.

At the base of our C2 pyramid are the physical needs for survival and good health: water, food, exercise, and appropriate veterinary care. With so many choices available today, a careful examination of each component of these physical needs is vital.

WATER, WATER EVERYWHERE

Dogs don't have a very good cooling system compared to that of humans. Our ability to sweat profusely is an exceedingly efficient way to regulate our body temperature. Although dogs do have a few sweat glands, mostly on their paw pads and around their noses, these glands seem to play a very small role, if any at all, in thermoregulation. Dogs rely primarily on panting to cool themselves. Normally, dogs breathe about thirty to forty times per minute, but a panting dog can breathe as rapidly as one hundred times or more in a minute. The moist tissues of dogs' upper respiratory tracts act as an evaporative surface, much like human skin, helping them dissipate heat. Water can mean the difference between life and death to an overheated dog.

Although hot weather does increase a dog's need for water, he needs approximately one-half to a full ounce of water per pound of body weight per day, regardless of the weather. So, a forty-eight-pound dog would need somewhere between four and six cups of water (1 to 1.5 liters) on a typical day, and potentially two or three times that amount when it is hot or the dog is exercising heavily. Some of that water will come from his food, but the majority will need to come from other sources. You can check your dog's hydration level by feeling his gums. If his gums are dry, he needs more water. If your dog has been sick and has dry gums, you need to let your veterinarian take a look at him. Dehydration in dogs, as in humans, is extremely serious and needs urgent treatment, usually with IV or subcutaneous fluids.

It is important to provide clean and safe water for dogs. It seems silly to say that, but we mess up on this one more than most people realize. Dogs need fresh water, whether they are inside or outside. Pool water is highly chlorinated and therefore unsafe for dogs. Additional outdoor sources of water can easily give your dog more than momentary refreshment: It can make him sick. Giardiasis is a protozoal infection that affects the small intestine. Any outdoor source of water, including puddles, creeks, rivers, and lakes, can contain giardia. This infection can cause diarrhea, weight loss, lethargy, and, if left untreated, permanent scarring of the small intestine. Although giardiasis is easily treated, it is even more easily prevented by keeping fresh water available for your dog in your yard and taking your own water with you when you go on excursions. Although uncommon, there is also the potential risk of zoonotic infection (diseases transmittable from animals to humans), especially in children who have close contact with a dog.

Taking your own water with you on outings is key. Communal bowls on city streets and in dog parks are simply infections waiting to happen, not just from waterborne diseases but also from other dogs' secretions that contain germs, such as those that cause kennel cough (*Bordetella*). Like treats, water has sparked many fights between thirsty dogs, so it is important to offer your dog a drink in a spot safely away from others. Also, some dogs may refuse to drink from strange water.

Finally, drinking from the toilet is not safe for your dog or for anyone your dog might lick. Even newly cleaned toilets can be full of bacteria. No matter how harmless this habit might seem, it is one you want to stop—immediately. In animal-owning households, all toilet lids should be kept closed.

Dogs can drink out of almost anything, but serious drinking is best done from a container wide enough to accommodate the dog's whole tongue plus a little wiggle room. Although most dogs make a scooping motion with their tongues to push water into their mouths, a lot of what's swallowed is actually bounced into their mouths by the lapping of their tongues.

Keep water bowls in several different rooms of the house, especially if you have more than one animal. Dogs don't usually guard water as a resource, but it is certainly possible if watering holes aren't plentiful. My pets have many water bowls, but they all take their postbreakfast drink from the same bowl in our bedroom. They wait in line, oldest to youngest. The cat, Bob, goes first. He tricks the dogs by pretending he is finished after every few licks. They all gear up to move forward in the line, and then Bob's little head goes back in the bowl. It is fascinating to me that three large dogs patiently wait for the cat to finish drinking. Then again, Bob can be fairly cranky.

DECIPHERING DOG FOOD

Water is relatively inexpensive; unfortunately, the same cannot be said of dog food. Pet food is a $15 billion-a-year industry, with a number of new dog foods hitting the shelves each year, scrambling to get a share of that lucrative market. It is hard to know which dog food is best for your dog—and also affordable.

The nutritional needs of an individual dog change with age and health, so no one food will be best for your dog's entire life. Likewise, each dog has unique nutritional needs, so one dog food might not be right for a multidog household. The label on a bag of dog food provides you with little usable information; it simply tells you that the food meets the minimum dog-food standards for protein and fat without too much fiber and moisture. "Minimum standards" are so low that there is an old joke saying you could put a boot, some motor oil, and a piece of cardboard into a blender, and the resulting slush would probably meet them. Labels don't tell you how much of the food is actually digestible; for that information, you must call the company. Look for digestibility above 80 percent—although good pet-food manufacturers have numbers greater than 90 percent.

Remember that if you compare canned food to dry kibble, you

are in essence comparing fresh apples, with all their moisture content, to dehydrated apples. For example, if dry puppy food contains no less than 28 percent protein per cup, you can expect that canned food, with high water content, will contain approximately 10 percent protein per cup. That doesn't mean, however, that your dog will take in a lower amount of protein on a daily basis—the labels will direct you to feed more canned food than dry. If you need to compare the total protein in a canned food with that of dry kibble, you will have to call the company and request "dry matter," or DM, values for both. DM is simply the content of a dog food when all moisture has been removed. If your dog has certain medical, or even behavioral, conditions, you absolutely must find out the true nutritional values of the food he is eating.

The sole exception to the useless-label rule is the phrase *complete and balanced*. This is a government-regulated claim, meaning the food contains adequate levels of all the nutrients that are essential for your dog's survival. Companies making this claim must be able to support it with data from either food trials or laboratory analysis. Actual food trials are far preferable to laboratory analysis, but any knowledge is more than some companies have.

Without exception, good, high-quality dog food has an 800 number listed on the bag so that you can call the company to ask questions about digestibility, DM nutrient percentages, and what, if any, testing trials have been done.

Marketing can cover a multitude of sins. Many companies list and advertise meat as the first, most plentiful ingredient in their dog food. In reality, most of these foods contain only approximately 3 percent meat. If they had a higher meat content, they would require refrigeration. Companies are able to get away with this because they break their plant proteins up into different components so that they can list meat as the most plenteous ingredient. They do this knowing owners often make two erroneous assumptions: Meat is the only acceptable form of protein, and dogs are carnivores.

In reality, dogs are omnivores, meaning they eat and thrive on both animal and vegetable matter. Although many of us like to perceive our dogs as the descendants of big, noble, thoroughly carnivorous gray wolves, mounting evidence indicates that the actual gray wolves from whom our dogs descended were much smaller creatures and more scavengers than hunters. Even the wolves of today start many of their meals with the gut of their prey, which likely contains grass and other vegetation.

All digestible protein, no matter the source, is good protein. Dogs would do quite well on a vegetarian diet as long as the vegetable proteins were complete (such as soy) or fed in appropriate combinations to form complete proteins. Ultimately, it doesn't matter that large, premium dog-food companies resort to clever marketing about meat being the primary ingredient. Most of them are simply telling us what we want to hear, while giving our dogs just what they need.

It's important to recognize that not all dog-food companies are created equal. As a matter of fact, many don't even manufacture their own product. Smaller companies simply formulate the recipe and send it off to be manufactured by another vendor. This is why so many different food companies, even upscale, boutique ones, are affected by major recalls. Remember the massive recall of dog and cat food because it contained contaminated protein from China? Melamine, a toxin that is not digestible in any form, had been added to boost the protein content. Much of the shipment went to a single manufacturing plant that makes numerous foods under various labels. It was a particularly frightening event, because many of those companies are respected, regulated food providers.

If dog food isn't shipped across state lines, it is not regulated—at all. A yummy-sounding formula could be created and sold regardless of its nutritional value or effect on dogs. Please be careful when you buy a chic, local brand of food. Although many low-cost dog foods are not very good for your dog, the same can be said of some very expensive brands. This is a buyer-beware market.

Purina, Royal Canin, Iams, and Hill's all manufacture their own food. This means that they have complete control over the safety and quality of ingredients that go into their products. Their diets are highly digestible because they use human-grade ingredients and have precise manufacturing and testing standards. These companies are also known as longtime leaders in veterinary nutritional research and supporters of research in universities and teaching hospitals. Company reputation is an important factor to consider when deciding on a food for your dog. Many of the less well-known (and less well-regarded) dog-food companies don't even have a veterinary nutritionist on staff.

Contrary to what you might think, when it comes to dog food, artificial preservatives aren't necessarily bad. Remember, dog food must contain preservatives, or it can be deadly for dogs. Synthetic preservatives stay stable during the manufacturing process, an important consideration. Natural preservatives tend to be altered during processing and therefore are not as effective at preserving food. Be careful about the storage and shelf life of any food with only natural preservatives. Unfortunately, natural preservatives are inexpensive and give smaller dog-food companies a trendy hook for attracting consumers.

At Canine Assistants, the cost of dog food is enormous, because we go through many tons each year. However, it is a cost we willingly pay, knowing that good food is so basic to a dog's health. We didn't always buy our dog food. In the days just before Kent, our veterinarian and my husband, came to Canine Assistants, a new boutique dog-food company donated food to us. The food was "all-natural and free of artificial preservatives." I felt almost smug about using it. Finally, our dogs were getting the kind of care they deserved.

One of Kent's first jobs as staff veterinarian was determining why all twenty of the dogs we had in training at the time had profuse vomiting and diarrhea. It took him about two minutes. The donated food was rancid.

Most of the claims about the dangers of certain synthetic preservatives stem from purely anecdotal evidence. Quality dog-food manufacturers, such as Purina, do extensive safety testing on all the ingredients they use. The last thing they want is to hurt your dog. That wouldn't be good for you, your dog, or the company's bottom line. Could we one day find out that a synthetic preservative used in dog food is toxic to dogs? It is possible, though extremely unlikely, based on the amount of testing these products have undergone to date. Still, it's true that we don't yet know everything about the long-term effects of every food our dogs eat.

We do, however, know what can happen when we feed rancid food to our dogs: They can die. And we can't always tell when food has gone bad. We may properly store and quickly use the all-natural dog food, but was the food handled properly during the lengthy manufacturing and shipping process? I'd prefer not to take the risk.

Home cooking isn't always the best option, either. Concerns over the past several years about the safety of our dogs' food, combined with our increasing view of dogs as family members, have led many to the idea of cooking their dogs' meals themselves. But it is difficult to create and maintain a balanced meal plan for dogs. The primary reason for this is something that nutritionists call "recipe drift." People have a tendency, over time, to make conscious or subconscious changes to a recipe. After multiple tiny changes, the diet might no longer meet the dog's nutritional requirements.

If you are truly committed to making your dog's food yourself, contact a veterinary nutritionist for assistance. Additionally, there is a website named Balance IT! (dvmconsulting.com) that will help you develop a diet that meets the needs of your dog based on breed, age, sex, medical conditions, and other factors. It will also tell you what add-ins are an absolute must. Although home cooking for dogs can be somewhat complicated, home *non*cooking can be a total disaster.

One of the most dangerous current fads is feeding a raw-meat diet to dogs. The so-called BARF—biologically appropriate raw foods—diet poses a serious health risk to your dog, your children, and you. An Australian veterinarian, Ian Billinghurst, designed the diet; his contention is that no species started out eating processed foods, including humans. Although this is absolutely true, we also didn't live very long. The ability to cook our meat so that it no longer contained bad microorganisms and parasites was a very positive step for humanity.

Why would we think it's healthful for our dogs to eat raw meat? Dogs can get salmonella, E. coli, campylobacter, and other deadly infectious agents from it. What makes this diet dangerous for people is that we buy chicken at the grocer's meat counter and then feed the raw chicken, along with salmonella, to our dogs. Then our dogs lick us and, whoops, we have salmonella. Both children and adults have reportedly died from this scenario. As one veterinarian I know says, "I wouldn't eat raw meat, and I wouldn't feed it to my dog, either."

Dogs do best with smaller meals multiple times per day. Dry kibble swells significantly in your dog's stomach after mixing with water and stomach acid, so large meals can be dangerous. Because I often use my dogs' kibble as a treat during the day and use meal-times as part of my teaching process, my dogs get very small meals four times per day. You might not be able or willing to do four meals, but strive for at least two or three. As for the amount, check the recommendation on your dog-food label, then feed your dog approximately two-thirds of that amount to start. Run your hands over your dog's rib cage at least once a week. If you can't easily feel his ribs, cut back on the amount you are giving him. If his ribs are very prominent, increase the amount. Dogs, when viewed from above, should show a clear waistline. Don't get stuck in the this-is-the-amount-I-always-feed-him rut. Be vigilant about the amount he actually needs.

It's always a bit startling to realize how little food dogs—even large ones—need to eat every day. The average dog requires twenty to twenty-five calories per pound of body weight per day. That number can go up to approximately forty calories per pound per day for active puppies and down to fifteen calories per pound per day for really sedentary dogs. Climate, exercise, age, personality, and other impacts on caloric intake all figure into the equation. But your average Rover weighing fifty pounds needs approximately one thousand calories per day. Dog food is extremely nutritious and calorie dense at approximately four hundred thirty calories per eight-ounce cup, so Rover would need a little more than two cups of food per day. If you despair over the idea of your dog eating so little, mix one cup of kibble with one cup of warm water and let it sit for thirty minutes or so. You will be surprised at how much the food expands. Soaking kibble is also a good way to slow down those dogs who "bolt" their food. But even if you serve it dry, the food will expand in your dog's stomach. Remember, a cup should be an eight-ounce portion, not your Big Gulp cup from 7-Eleven. Our failure to accurately measure food is one of the most common reasons our dogs become overweight.

Try not to feed people food to your dog, because it can confuse the calorie-versus-nutrition ratio. People food can also be difficult on your dog's stomach, causing such horrors as pancreatitis. Small amounts of simple but delicious human food, such as cheese or peanut butter, can be used in a teaching context when needed.

Quality commercial treats, such as Milk-Bones, do meet some of your dog's nutritional needs, so using these treats rather than people food is more healthful and probably safer for your dog's stomach. At Canine Assistants, there are times when we must bring out the extraordinary treats such as cheese, peanut butter, and low-fat cuts of cooked meat to properly motivate the dogs. Remember that treats are not designed to replace food, so consider using kibble as your standard treat and bringing out the big yums only when you truly need them.

Keeping your dog at a healthful weight is the kindest thing you can do for him. Obesity is the number-one health problem in American dogs, affecting some 35 to 45 percent of them. Obesity in dogs increases their risk of serious orthopedic conditions such as hip dysplasia, cruciate-ligament injuries, arthritis, and back problems. It also increases your dog's risk of certain cancers, heart disease, diabetes, liver disease, heatstroke, and respiratory problems. As if that weren't enough, obese dogs have a greater risk of surgical complications. There are some "light" formula dog foods available commercially, but to my knowledge, the most effective weight-loss diets are available only by prescription. It's a good idea to involve your veterinarian if your dog is significantly overweight, so she can keep a close eye on your dog's health. A medical problem such as hypothyroidism or diabetes might be causing your dog to gain (or be unable to lose) weight. Don't be embarrassed: Many of us, myself included, have struggled to keep a dog at an appropriate weight.

EXERCISE

People often ask me how I feel about dogs being kept in urban housing without access to a fenced yard. I feel good about it. Dogs who have to be leash-walked tend to get more exercise than dogs who are merely turned out into a fenced yard. Those of us with big fenced yards like to imagine our dogs joyfully scurrying around, getting plenty of exercise, but the truth is most dogs who go out alone just amble a bit, do their business, and return to the back door. It is a rare dog who will exercise himself.

How much exercise a dog needs depends on his age, his breed, and his current fitness level. A good rule of thumb is that a dog should exercise at least once a day for long enough to noticeably slow down in his energy level. Be sure to watch your dog closely for fatigue. Panting is a good indicator: A little is healthy, a lot can signal danger. Be careful in warm weather if exercising outdoors, because some dogs, especially heavy-coated northern breeds, are susceptible to heat-related problems. Avoid encouraging your dog to do quick turning maneuvers, especially on slick floors; this will protect his knees. Additionally, be careful about his running on certain surfaces, such as tennis courts, because they can tear up your dog's paw pads.

Although it can be difficult to find ways to exercise your dog indoors if weather or other circumstances prevent outdoor activities, it is not impossible. One of our Canine Assistants recipients exercises his big Lab by throwing a ball down a hall so the dog can run the ball back to him. Another plays hide-and-seek with her dog indoors and out. A third has a squeaky toy attached to a kid's fishing rod for her dog to chase.

Freestyle dancing with dogs has recently become a popular exercise option. You can find videos online that will provide creative ideas for choreography. Some dogs love to play basketball, indoors or out. You can play monkey-in-the-middle by throwing a ball back and forth with another person as your dog chases it. If no one else is available, you can play by throwing the ball against a wall. Either way, you should let your dog intercept the ball often enough to keep him interested. Let your dog do puppy push-ups by having him rapidly repeat "Sit, Down, Sit." Make his workout harder by having him do "Stand, Down, Stand." You can set up mini obstacle courses using Hula-hoops as jumps and broomsticks as limbo poles. Use your creativity, and you'll find exercise opportunities anywhere.

Obviously, varying your dog's form of exercise keeps things more interesting for both of you, but don't worry if that's difficult. Just get your dog up and moving. Dogs who love certain activities such as chasing balls or squeaky toys seem content to repeat them day after day.

BEING PREPARED

Hurricane Katrina reminded us of the importance of being prepared to care for our animals in the event of emergencies. It's a good idea to put together a canine survival kit, including the following items:

- a two-week supply of food in an airtight, waterproof container
- a few toys and treats your dog particularly likes
- a two-week supply of bottled water (Note: Water that is not safe for people is not safe for your dog.)
- a two-week supply of your dog's medications
- several collapsible bowls
- cleanup bags
- an extra leash and collar
- brush, toothbrush, toothpaste
- a collapsible crate
- an envelope containing all your dog's personal and medical information

In addition, post stickers on all doors to your home alerting emergency workers to the number and species of all animal residents.

Keep the number for your dog's regular veterinarian, your preferred veterinary emergency facility, and the Animal Poison Control

Center (888-426-4435). There is a charge for calling, but it is well worth the cost. When calling the center, be ready to provide relevant information about your pet, including his weight, age, symptoms, the substance and amount ingested, and when it happened.

Every dog owner should keep a basic first-aid kit for home treatment of minor ailments, containing the following items:

gauze
nonstick bandages
strips of clean cloth
adhesive tape (Don't use Band-Aids on your dog.)
milk of magnesia
activated charcoal
3 percent hydrogen peroxide
sterile saline solution
a digital fever thermometer (Fever thermometers measure
    higher temperatures than standard thermometers.)
large syringe without needle
necktie or thigh-high stocking, for use as a muzzle
flashlight
tweezers
styptic pen or powder
antibiotic ointment, such as Neosporin
Benadryl
Betadine or similar surgical disinfectant
scissors

FIRST AID FOR YOUR DOG

One of the most important things you can do to safeguard your pet's health is to know what constitutes *normal* for your dog. A dog's normal body temperature ranges from 100 to 102.5°F at rest. A dog's pulse can easily be felt on his leg at approximately the point where his left elbow would touch his chest cavity. At rest, dogs younger than one year of age should have a pulse between 120 and 160 beats per minute; adult dogs weighing less than thirty pounds should have a pulse between 100 and 160 beats per minute; dogs weighing more than thirty pounds should have a pulse between 60 and 100 beats per minute. Dogs have a respiration rate of ten to thirty breaths per minute. When panting, their respiration can go up to more than 100 breaths per minute.

Check your dog's normal pulse and respiration so you have a baseline for later comparison if needed. Keep a written journal recording these values, dated for reference. Recheck every six to twelve months, because normal values can change over time. If you notice a steady increase in these control values over a period of time, mention it to your veterinarian at your next appointment to make sure the change doesn't indicate a problem.

Check your dog's normal gum color for future reference. This is extremely important (standard coloration varies widely with the individual), because changes in gum color can alert you to the seriousness of an internal problem. If your dog has mostly black gums, you will have to hunt for a spot of pink. Pale gums in an ill or injured dog might mean that his blood pressure is low. Brick-red gums might be a sign of increased blood pressure, sepsis, or dehydration. Remember that dry gums also indicate dehydration in dogs. If you are unable to rehydrate a dehydrated dog, get him to the vet as quickly as possible. This is especially true if he is experiencing fluid loss from vomiting or diarrhea. If he is losing fluids and is unable to keep water down or in, he needs immediate veterinary attention.

It is also important to know how to check your dog's capillary refill time (CRT). Capillaries are the tiny blood vessels that compose the vascular bed between arteries and veins. To check your dog's CRT, press your fingertip firmly on a pink spot of gum for five seconds, then remove your finger and see how long it takes for the color to once again match that of the surrounding tissue. In most dogs, CRT is approximately 1.5 seconds. Slow CRT can be another indicator of low blood pressure. If your dog is sick and you can easily see a difference in his gum color or his CRT, this warrants an urgent visit to your veterinarian.

Giving your dog appropriate first aid can mean the difference between life and death for him. See Appendix A for instructions on handling some common veterinary emergencies. In addition, I urge you to check with your veterinarian or local Red Cross to find a nearby class on first aid for animals. Nothing beats seeing techniques demonstrated and practicing them with the guidance of a qualified instructor.

CHAPTER FOUR

Veterinary Health

In the early days of Canine Assistants, I was headed to North Carolina to do some recurrent follow-up training with one of our service dogs and his recipient. Just as I boarded the plane, powerful thunderstorms developed over the Atlanta airport, and the plane was held for more than an hour. To pass the time, the flight attendants began playing a game with the passengers. They would ask a trivia question, and the first passenger to ring his call button and supply the correct answer won some fabulous prize, such as a bag of pretzels or a box of tissues. One question was, "What cleans teeth and freshens breath but isn't mouthwash, mints, gum, or toothpaste?" Unfair advantage for me . . . Milk-Bones! I won a roll of toilet paper.

I was up one roll of toilet paper for the trip, but it cost me any chance of a quiet, peaceful flight. The woman next to me immediately asked, "So, are you a dog person? Do you know anything about dogs? I have a dog. His name is Punkin. He's a papillon. Do you know anything about papillons? He has terrible breath. Would Milk-Bones help? I have to find something because Mommy can't kiss her little Punkin while he has stinky breath. Should I try those chew sticks for teeth? I mean not me, obviously, but should I give one to Punkin?" All of that came out before she paused to take a breath. I remember thinking, *What incredible lung capacity this woman has.*

As it turns out, she was a singer, who did indeed have amazing lungs. But she was also a world-class talker and never stopped long enough for me to answer her questions. I would have said, "Punkin needs to be seen by a good veterinarian."

FINDING THE RIGHT VET

Have you ever thought, "I wish my dog's vet could be *my* doctor?" What is it about good veterinarians that makes us love them so much? At least in part, it is because your veterinarian probably acts as your dog's first-line internist, surgeon, orthopedist, dentist, ophthalmologist, and anesthesiologist, so you likely see more of him than you do your own physician.

When I was twelve years old, my family needed to find a new veterinarian for our dog, and by good fortune, we were introduced to Dr. Hines, a wonderful man with an uncanny intuition about animals. From the first day, Dr. Hines was like a member of the family, and we knew he could be trusted. Not only was he smart and caring, but his office was located less than five minutes from our house. But when he moved his practice some forty-five minutes away, there was never a question about what we would do—we followed him. Whenever our dog required care, we would trek the forty-five minutes to see Dr. Hines. My mother used to say she would have followed him from Atlanta to Seattle if she had to.

Such a wonderful relationship with a veterinarian was not always the case with our family. One day, just before Dr. Hines entered the scene, our dog, Daphne, came limping in from the yard on a swollen back leg. My older sister Lisa, who was seventeen at the time, was babysitting us. She bundled Daphne and me into the car and took us to the local veterinarian. Daphne was a fear biter and, consequently, not a good patient. Lisa was very clear in telling the new vet that Daphne would bite when stressed and should be sedated or muzzled. He ignored her completely, and of course Daphne bit him on the thumb. It broke the skin, and I'm certain that it hurt, but what he did in response was horrible. He began choking Daphne to the point of semiconsciousness, saying with loud authority that it would calm her. My sister pleaded with him to stop, and finally he released his hold. The vet assured us that the choking was standard procedure. I was not convinced. He was angry and taking his emotions out on a small, very scared dog. I had nightmares about that man for months. They stopped when I met Dr. Hines.

How do you find a Dr. Hines of your own? Recommendations from friends who share your affection and commitment to dogs is the best way. When you get a lead on a good veterinarian, call and make an appointment to meet her without your dog (because the majority of new veterinarians are female, I will use the feminine pronoun). Get to your appointment early, and watch how the office runs. Chaos is okay—every clinic gets a little crazy from time to time. Unkindness to pets or their owners is not. Veterinarians, as do most people, tend to hire those whose personalities appeal to them. If the front-office staff is rude, chances are the back office will not be any better. Dr. Hines had one employee when we first began seeing him. Her name was Barbara, and I once told my mom that I wanted to grow up to be just like her. I still do.

Don't dismiss the idea of using a relatively recent graduate as your veterinarian, as long as she is willing to request help, when in doubt, from more experienced colleagues. Ask at what point she generally consults with or refers patients to specialists when dealing with a difficult case. If she doesn't seem comfortable with the idea of soliciting help, this is probably not the veterinarian for you. No one person can know everything.

Ask what sort of pain management she would use for a painful procedure. The veterinarian should recognize that, although dogs may not always yelp, they do feel pain. The notion and practice of pain management has been slow in coming to small-animal veterinary medicine, but thankfully, it has finally arrived. Managing pain is now part of standard care for all animals. As with humans, suffering delays healing and has a detrimental effect on overall health. Some practitioners will be more focused on pain management than others, so be prepared to advocate on your dog's behalf if you feel he needs better pain control for acute situations, such as after surgery, or for chronic conditions, including arthritis.

You need to know what the clinic's policy is on emergencies. Most urban clinics send patients to emergency specialists after hours. This is a good thing. Your veterinarian can't be at her office all the time. But be sure the veterinarian sounds as if she remains involved in your dog's healthcare no matter the circumstances and is available to consult with specialists as needed.

Go with your gut. Do you like this person? She is going to be in charge of the well-being of your precious dog, so be certain you can envision yourself working well with her. If the clinic is a large, multi-vet practice, be certain it is reasonably possible to see this one practitioner for most things. Large practices are fine, even good in some ways, but you don't want to see someone different at each visit. Make sure your veterinarian of choice takes appointments or will otherwise arrange to care for your dog individually as much as possible.

When you feel that you have found your perfect match, ask about office hours. Is the clinic open on Saturdays or late in the evening during the week? Ask what times seem to be best for routine appointments and what you can do in preparation for your visit. Find out their fee schedules, but don't become too focused on how much a clinic charges. Check around to see that their fees are in line with other clinics', but don't make this the sole factor in choosing your dog's doctor. If your budget is tight, explain this to the vet and see what she says. Good vets will hear you and understand that it is important they keep costs down. Even in large practices, there are usually things that a veterinarian can and will do to help if money is genuinely tight. Vets want clients who care. But be fair. Don't pay the vet clinic last just because your veterinarian is kind and understanding. Having worked with veterinarians, I can tell you firsthand how demoralizing it is to see someone who professes not to have enough money to pay a bill driving away in an expensive new car.

Once you have selected a veterinarian, be sure you show your appreciation to the clinic for the care they take of your dog. Being kind to the front-office staff is as important as to the veterinarian

herself. Many times I have seen people be abusive with the recep-
tionist or technician and then perfectly charming with the veterinarian. Any good vet will be very sensitive to the way you treat her
staff. And, because I have worked in clinics, trust me when I say that
these support people are extremely important to your dog's care.
They are the ones who will hold and comfort your dog, and although most people who work in clinics are genuinely nice, the
animals belonging to favorite clients tend to get a little extra love
from them. It's simply human nature.

Be sensitive about requesting second opinions. If you are dealing with something difficult, ask your vet if she has had a similar
case. Inquire if there is anyone else who might be a good additional
resource. If you have the overwhelming desire to sneak your dog off
to the other clinic down the street, you aren't with the right vet in
the first place. Veterinarians get hurt feelings, just like anyone else.
If you don't want to damage your relationship, tell her that you
would certainly understand if she wanted to bring in some help but
you hope she will remain in charge, or at least active, with the case.

Although you want to honor your veterinarian's role in your
dog's healthcare, it is critical to have the same respect *from* your vet.
If you don't feel that she is taking your concerns seriously, even after
you have clearly repeated them, you need to seek help elsewhere. If
there is any chance your dog's well-being is at risk, do not worry
about your vet's feelings—do what you must.

One of our Canine Assistants recipients had a lovely dog from
another organization as his first assistance dog. He used a walking
harness to assist him with balance. One day, he realized that his dog
was lame, sensing it through the harness. His veterinarian couldn't
find anything wrong, suggested he was probably sore from the harness, and recommended rest. That explanation seemed reasonable,
and the man took his dog home. But the lameness persisted. Still the
veterinarian found nothing. By the time everyone could actually see
the dog's lameness, bone cancer had spread so extensively that treatment was no longer viable.

The veterinarian might be your dog's doctor, but as a good
owner, you are your dog's best advocate. Ask for a referral to a spe-

cialty practice or university if you feel that something is being missed. Large specialty clinics tend to be significantly more pleasant for the human client than a university veterinary medical center. Appointment times are more readily available, even if services will possibly be more expensive. It is unlikely that anyone will offer you a latte at a university facility. However, it is common at a university to have to describe your dog's case repeatedly—first to a student, then to an intern, then to a resident, and finally to the clinician in charge. That can be frustrating. That said, keep in mind that sometimes having the opportunity to repeat information helps you remember important facts that you might have overlooked if you just ran through it once. And each of those people will be doing everything in their power to help your dog. Of the four levels of staff, it is the student who is the most likely to crawl into your dog's crate to snuggle and be the first to answer your calls, so be tolerant and kind.

With our Canine Assistants dogs-in-training, we refer to a local specialty practice where there are wonderful surgeons, internists, and other specialty practitioners. But if one of my own dogs required a surgical procedure so specialized that my husband didn't feel comfortable handling it himself, I would immediately head to one of our nearby vet schools, where I know several brilliant veterinarians. And my husband would likely be driving; good vets know when to ask for help.

PET INSURANCE

As advancements in veterinary medicine have increased, so have the costs associated with better treatments. This trend has led to a growth in the pet-insurance industry. There are a number of good insurance policies available these days, and if you choose to insure your dog, keep the following things in mind as you decide which company and which policy will best meet your needs.

- Do you want coverage for routine and preventative care, such as annual vaccinations, or are you primarily concerned about unexpected accidents and injuries? Your monthly premium should be substantially lower if you choose to carry coverage for only major medical issues.

- Some policies do not allow you to choose your own veterinarians. Is that important to you? (It is to me!)
- What deductible and what monthly payment works best for your cash flow?
- What exactly will the policy cover? Are riders an option for things such as preexisting conditions? Are breed-specific genetic conditions covered, such as the hip dysplasia common in Labs or German shepherds?
- Will the benefit amount cover the actual expense? Compare your veterinarian's fees to the insurance company's benefits for common procedures.
- Does the company increase your premiums as your dog ages? If so, is the amount of the increase fixed?
- When, how, and to whom (you or the veterinarian) are benefits paid?
- Are there discounts for multiple pets?

Because no one wants to make life-or-death decisions about her pet on a purely monetary basis, I urge you to investigate insurance coverage before you need it. If you choose to forgo insurance, set aside money every month in an animal-care fund so that it is available when needed for emergencies.

PUPPY CARE

As I write this, we have puppies due at Canine Assistants. Even though we've had an average of ten litters per year for the past fourteen years, I am always excited when puppies are coming. I think about the people they will help and what extraordinary lives they will lead. This particular litter is extra-special to me. My dog Butch is the dad, and the mom dog is Louise, one of my all-time favorite girls.

Our breeder dogs live with volunteer families. Moms come to the Canine Assistants facility a few days before their puppies are due and stay until they are weaned. The puppies are born in our vet clinic under my husband's desk, because that is where the moms seem to feel most comfortable. Mother dogs are bred approximately once a year, a maximum of four times. I love all the dogs at Canine Assistants, but I revere our moms. They are my heroes.

Although not many people will be responsible for their dogs before the dogs are at least eight weeks old, it's important to know a little bit about the early days of a puppy's life.

Mother dogs can be bred approximately twice a year, and most veterinarians feel it's acceptable to breed every heat—especially when these are seven to eight months apart. Most breeders give Mom a cycle off after two litters, or breed every other heat. Gestation is sixty-three days, beginning at ovulation. Litter size can vary from as small as one pup to as large as fifteen. In general, toy breeds have litters of two to four pups, medium breeds four to six, and large breeds seven to nine. Giant breeds often have more than nine puppies. Although the average litter size registered with the American Kennel Club (AKC) is seven for golden and Labrador retrievers, we have had litters at Canine Assistants from as small as a single puppy to as large as fourteen. Our litter average is eight.

In utero, each puppy has its own placenta in a Y-shaped uterus. The long arms of the Y are known as the uterine horns, and the shorter base is called the uterine body. Eighty percent of the time, puppies are born from alternating horns, so it is common to have one puppy born within a few minutes of the next. Approximately 60 percent of puppies are born headfirst, with the remainder coming out rump-first. Moms do not seem to have any more difficulty delivering either way.

Although sometimes puppies can arrive in quick succession, there can also be long intervals between births. Natural delivery of a litter usually takes between six and twelve hours. At Canine Assistants, we like to see an average of at least one puppy per hour. However, there are times when moms get tired or puppies get stuck, and a cesarian section (C-section) is necessary. For some breeds, planned C-sections are the norm, but our moms typically deliver naturally. I always feel somewhat sorry for first-time moms who have a C-section to deliver all their puppies, waking to find small creatures surrounding her. In any case, nature quickly takes over in the moms, and even first-timers usually handle their puppies like seasoned veterans.

Puppies, like all animals, still have much developing to do once they are born. The developmental stages of puppies are divided by age. Although we will consider the physical development and health needs of puppies by age here, I will talk later about the social needs of puppies during these same periods.

Neonatal Period (Days 0–10)

Newborn puppies are working on sensory development during the first ten days of their lives. They are born quite prematurely from a developmental perspective and thus are entirely dependent on their mom. When puppies are born, their eyes are closed; their hearing is very poor; and they can't yet sit, stand, or walk. Puppies at this age have to be stimulated by their mamas to defecate and urinate. Their movement is limited to an inefficient form of crawling.

At this point, puppies do not have a fully functioning immune system and are very susceptible to infectious diseases. Even bacteria that cause no problems for adult dogs can kill pups via septicemia. In addition, puppies at this stage cannot regulate their own body temperature. Mom does a good job of keeping them warm, but it helps to keep them in a temperature-controlled environment. During the neonatal period, a puppy's normal body temperature is 96–98°F.

About the only things puppies of this age can do is suckle, raise their heads, root their noses, and right themselves if they get turned over—the skills needed to nurse.

At Canine Assistants, our Number 1 Rule of Raising Pups is *Take care of Mom: She's doing all the work.* Moms need three times their normal caloric intake to produce enough milk to properly nurture their pups. We keep a constant eye on Mom's temperature, mammary glands, water consumption, and appetite during this period of puppy development.

The puppies mostly sleep, waking to nurse every two to three hours. They can lose body weight slightly the day after birth; thereafter, puppies should gain 5–10 percent daily and double their birth weight by two weeks of age. It is important that puppies nurse within their first twelve hours to absorb colostrum, which contains important antibodies. After twenty-four hours, all antibody absorption ceases. Colostrum-deprived pups are more disease susceptible.

Because veterinarians do not know the quality of a particular mom's colostrum, and consequently the level of her pups' immunity, puppies receive multiple vaccinations between six and sixteen weeks of age. Furthermore, vets have no way of determining when the maternal antibodies have declined enough to allow the puppies' immune systems to respond, producing antibodies for themselves. Therefore, the puppies are vaccinated three to four times to ensure all potentialities are covered. Early shots protect those puppies who did not receive proper colostrum levels. Conversely, late shots cover those who received extra quantities of colostrum, which slowed the puppies' immune systems from developing antibodies to disease agents.

Transitional Period (Days 10–21)

Pups next work on motor-skill development, while their dependency on Mom begins to decrease. Much happens during this stage. Puppies' eyes and ear canals generally open at between ten and fourteen days, although at day 5, hearing begins to improve even through partially closed canals. Still, primarily due to neurologic development, full hearing isn't possible until the canals are completely open.

By ten to fourteen days, most puppies are good crawlers, their front legs able to support weight. Between eleven and fifteen days, their rear legs also strengthen enough to support weight. By sixteen days, puppies can vocalize other than crying, and at eighteen, pups typically have a startle reflex to loud stimuli.

By twenty-one days, all puppies should be good walkers, and their pain perception is normally fully developed. They can now defecate and urinate on their own, and their suckle reflex begins to disappear.

Socialization Period (Three Weeks to Three Months)

Most puppies begin eating solid food in the third or fourth week of life, and at approximately the fourth week, they learn to climb. By this time they can fully regulate their own body temperature and their vision is more highly developed, but it isn't as sharp and clear as an adult dog's until approximately eight weeks of age.

Mother dogs typically wean their pups between the fourth and fifth weeks. This is largely because the puppies' deciduous incisors begin to erupt at four weeks, quickly followed by canine teeth and premolars . . . a painful development for Mom.

Juvenile Period (Three to Eight Months)

Puppies are usually fully vaccinated by four months of age and are generally spayed or neutered sometime before the end of this period. The decision to spay or neuter your dog is an important one. If you are not a dedicated breeder, do not let your dog have puppies. In chapter 9, you will find a more complete discussion of this issue, with a list of the pros and cons of altering your dog.

Vaccinations and Deworming

Every veterinarian has her preferred schedule for puppy vaccinations and deworming. Here is an example of a good protocol.

PUPPY'S AGE (IN WEEKS)	TREATMENT NEEDED
6	distemper, deworming (given every two weeks until sixteen weeks of age), fecal check, heartworm preventive begins
9	distemper, parvo, coronavirus, *Bordetella*
12	distemper, parvo, coronavirus, Lyme (two-shot series)
16	distemper, parvo, coronavirus, rabies, fecal flotation, Lyme

After thirteen or fourteen months, long-bone growth is complete, and dogs are considered adults in terms of physical development.

OLDER DOGS

Puppies and young adults are not the only dogs who have special veterinary concerns. I recently sent this letter to the supporters of Canine Assistants, appealing for help with a veterinary need.

We have a dog, and a boy, in desperate need of your help. Delilah is a 10-year-old Black Lab who has worked for the past eight and a half years with a wonderful young man named Matthew who has cerebral palsy. There aren't words to explain how important Delilah is to this young man. She is part of him, body and soul. She has allowed him to function in a world where the odds were stacked against him from the moment he was born.

Now, the odds are stacked against Delilah. She has been diagnosed with a mass on her spleen. The mass could be cancerous or it could be totally benign. We won't know until Delilah undergoes an expensive surgery to remove her spleen. If it is cancer, the veterinary oncologist believes that treatment can still buy her significant time. If it is benign, Delilah could have years of life remaining. There are times, when a condition is so advanced or pervasive, that treatment simply isn't fair to the dog and the kindest thing we can do is let go. This is not one of those times.

I promised when I started this program that we would move heaven and earth if one of our dogs needed this type of medical treatment. We even established a fund called the Zoe Fund, named in memory of a very special dog, for just such emergencies. The problem is the money isn't there right now to pay for the surgery. Funding has been very tight for us for the past few years, as it has been for everyone.

In this Season of Giving, I can't think of a greater gift than more time for Delilah and Matthew. Please consider a donation to Canine Assistants' Zoe Fund. A boy and his dog need you.

Most people were very kind in response to the letter, but one man was incensed that I would ask for money to help a ten-year-old dog. I calmly explained that old age isn't a disease; it is a part of life. Just because a dog is older, it doesn't mean you shouldn't provide the highest possible level of care. It is a sad, horrible fact that 25 percent of the dogs turned in to shelters are given up because they are "too old." Older dogs are awesome. They let you sleep late. They know the routine. True, dogs don't live forever, but that is all the more reason we should make every day as wonderful as possible for them.

IN THE END

It is a dreadful fact of life that most of our dogs will die before us. And worse, many will need us to make the end-of-life decision for them. You have loved and nurtured this animal, so how do you know when it's time to let go, and when euthanasia is appropriate? The answer involves both *your dog's physical* and *your mental* health. There will come a day when, looking into your dog's eyes, you will know that it's time to let him go.

The ability to release our dogs from pain through euthanasia is both a great gift and an almost unbearable burden. However, my personal and professional experience has been surprisingly positive. I have worked in veterinary clinics and seen the process from a clinical point of view; I have made the decision to let my own dogs go when their suffering seemed unrelenting; and I have been with family and friends as they made the same difficult determination. Although the physical process of dying has always seemed to be a peaceful experience for the animals, for the people who love them it is often another story entirely.

There is a difference between *pain* and *suffering.* Pain is treatable with a number of medications, some of which are extremely effective and can significantly improve a dog's quality of life. In my experience, failure to eat and social withdrawal are the two primary signs that an elderly or infirm animal may be suffering and approaching the end of his life. Remember that a brief period (one or two days) of not eating or socializing does not necessarily mean the end is near. Give your dog some time to be sure, because dogs, like people, have good days and bad days. I refer to this evaluation period as the "eat-and-greet assessment." When you are certain that your dog has had adequate pain medication but shows no real pleasure in seeing you and refuses to eat, it is time to talk to your veterinarian about euthanasia.

Although euthanasia is a gift we can offer our dogs when they are suffering, it should never be used as a matter of convenience. Many people ask veterinarians to euthanize healthy dogs because they, their owners, are no longer able or willing to care for them. Your moving from a house to an apartment should not be a death sentence for your dog, nor should your dog's unwanted barking. Ask your veterinary clinic for help in rehoming your dog or in managing behavior issues, but do not ask its staff to put your dog to sleep solely because that dog has become an inconvenience.

As previously noted, some veterinarians are more sensitive to pain management than others. A good, responsive vet will make end-of-life care easier for you and your dog. If your current D.V.M. is not receptive to your concerns, ask to be referred to a pain specialist. With adequate pain control, some dogs have gained six months or more, when it previously seemed euthanasia was imminent.

Several years ago, Honey, my friend Maggie's golden retriever, was diagnosed with inoperable cancer. Honey had always been an energetic, fun-loving dog but had begun to refuse walks and food, and even seemed unresponsive to Maggie's presence. Maggie was distraught by what was happening to her best friend and begged her vet for help. The vet prescribed pain patches, and Honey slept for nearly two days, waking only for water and the occasional bathroom break. Maggie, unaware that sedation is a side effect of most narcotics, was sure that Honey's condition had irreversibly deteriorated and the end was near. Amazingly, on the third morning, Honey woke up, barked for breakfast, and then ran outside for the first time in months. The pain was finally under control. The relief Honey experienced undoubtedly allowed her to sleep peacefully for the first time in many days. For nearly six months Maggie kept the patches on her beloved dog, until the day came when it was clear that time had run out. To this day, Maggie is grateful for those six months and the quality of life Honey experienced up until the end.

Clearly, Honey's intense pain was causing her to suffer. She didn't try to get up or wag her tail when Maggie came in the door and would not eat—not even steak. The patches alleviated the pain, giving her and Maggie precious time together. But when the end arrives, if you need a few days to come to terms with your decision, that's understandable. I strongly suspect, were your dog able to understand, that he would tell you the same thing. Just do your best to make him comfortable.

When it's time to say final goodbyes, your presence might not always ease your dog's mind. Instinctually, he may realize that it's his time to go, but it's unlikely that he connects his impending death with this visit to the veterinarian. If you want to be present, hold yourself together, or stay away until the sedative has been given. I have always struggled with this holding-yourself-together thing, so I understand the difficulty. However, emotional instability might increase your dog's stress level—not a good thing at a time like this. By this point, your dog is likely comfortable with veterinary procedures, but your emotion might be upsetting to him. If it is not possible to keep your emotions in check, ask a friend to be with your dog. But, most likely, no matter who is present, even if it's the clinic staff alone, your dog will be in caring hands. Don't allow anyone (including yourself) to make you feel guilty if you cannot be present when your dog is euthanized. The bottom line is that your dog would want you to handle this in the way that makes you feel best. After all, he loves you.

Unfortunately, there will be one more difficult decision to make once your dog has passed away: what to do with your pet's body. Veterinary clinics can handle the arrangements, or you can make your own. Many local laws prohibit burying pets on private property. Although pet cemeteries are becoming increasingly common, cremation is also a popular option these days, because many people like the idea of keeping their dog's remains.

But the dogs we love never leave us, regardless of what happens to their physical bodies. They are there when we fall asleep at night, ever vigilant. They are there when we wake, helping us live another day, joyous in the fact that we have known and given love. They stand quietly beside us when we open our hearts to a new dog, secure in the knowledge that their goodness made us better.

As for sweet Delilah, I sent out the following letter shortly after my initial request for financial assistance.

Dear Friends,
Several weeks ago, we asked you to help us fund urgent surgery for a wonderful Lab named Delilah who had been diagnosed with a large, bleeding mass on her spleen. We knew going into the surgery that the vast majority of bleeding splenetic masses are cancerous of the most aggressive sort. We also knew that Delilah and her dad, Matthew, deserved every possible chance for more time together. So, we asked for your help and forged ahead.

Guess what? THE TUMOR WAS BENIGN! Delilah made it through the surgery without any problems and is back with her boy where she belongs. Her prognosis is great. It was a miracle that wouldn't have happened without your help. Thank you. You saved two lives, those of Delilah and Matthew.

Sometimes you win one.

CHAPTER FIVE

Safe Havens

She arrived at Canine Assistants in the hatchback of a Honda Civic, a pitiful sack of bones loosely arranged into a young Labrador. The driver of the Honda explained that she had just witnessed a man throw the dog from the bed of a pickup truck. The first thing we noticed was that her tail, wagging furiously, and her tongue, gently licking the hand of her rescuer, were still operational, but most of the rest of her was not. A physical exam showed that she was thin, dehydrated, scraped, bruised, and completely unable to stand on her back legs. Radiographs revealed a badly broken pelvis. Through all the tests, her tail never stopped wagging, and she never stopped kissing anyone who came within range. We named her Grace.

Plentiful food, clean water, good vet care, and time healed Grace's body, and as she regained her strength, she began to display a high level of intelligence and an almost uncanny knack for scent detection. One day, to keep her mind occupied while she was on exercise restriction, I taught Grace how to use her nose to roll one of the red rubber balls that we kept in a large bin. She was a remarkably quick learner. The next day, I again reached into the bin and pulled out one of the many red rubber balls, but when I rolled it to Grace, she ignored it completely, staring intently at the bin. Because she could not move, I dragged the entire storage box over to Grace, tilting it so she could stick her nose inside without having to stand. Immediately, she began rooting through the thirty or so identical balls. After several seconds, she grabbed one in her mouth, dropped it on the ground and nosed it toward me. Grace didn't want just any ball; she wanted the same ball we'd played with the previous day.

I couldn't see the difference, but she could smell it, a display of extraordinary scenting skills. I asked my contacts at U.S. Customs and Border Protection (CBP) if they would like to test her as a potential drug- or bomb-detection dog when she was completely healed. She passed their tests easily and was taken to the CBP training center in Virginia.

Grace now spends her days searching for bombs on the Israeli border. I've heard she is excellent at her job. Grace's whole life is dedicated to keeping people, the same species who once let her down so badly, safe. When I first heard of her job, I wondered if she would still do it if she understood the danger. Then I recalled the first time I saw her—how she wagged her tail and licked the woman's hand—and I knew the answer. Such is the way of dogkind.

Dogs have been protecting humans for as long as dogs have existed. The superior sensory skills of canids have provided those of us with lesser sensory abilities great comfort. When I was a little girl, I had my dog check my bedroom for monsters and other potential threats. Even then, I knew that she was the member of my family most likely to detect any prospective problems. It seems many people instinctively recognize that dogs offer their protection to those whom they love.

This protection connection between humans and dogs can be seen in Seattle, one of my favorite stops on the tour for *Through a Dog's Eyes*. It is an extremely dog-friendly city. Our hotel featured special guest rooms for those traveling with dogs, complete with dog beds, bowls, and a variety of wonderful treats. Butch, who was with me on tour, would certainly vote Seattle one of his favorite stops. He spent much of his time conning the hotel's housekeeping staff out of extra treats.

The number of homeless people in Seattle who have large, scary-looking dogs astonished me. Even more amazing is that the dogs look significantly healthier than their people. My superb media escort explained that those who lived on the streets used the dogs for personal protection and that most of these individuals would gladly go hungry before allowing their dogs to do so. "The dogs," she said, "keep their people safe, and the people make a valiant effort to reciprocate."

IN THE AFTERMATH

She's a blond bombshell, the type you typically associate with heiress party girls who float through a crowd with the confidence that comes with constant attention. But one look in her eyes suggests she's far more than a pretty face. She is a golden retriever, a search-and-rescue (SAR) dog named Puzzle, one of a special group of dogs that help rescue those already caught by disaster.

I knew of this little golden long before I met her. Puzzle's mom, Susannah Charleson, wrote the remarkable book *Scent of the Missing,* detailing Puzzle's development as a SAR dog. When I discovered that Susannah and I had both been invited to speak at an event in South Florida, I was delighted.

Butch and I were on the same plane from Atlanta to West Palm Beach as Susannah and Puzzle, though we couldn't see one another. My first glimpse of them wasn't until we reached baggage claim. Susannah is a dark-haired beauty with a peaceful, reassuring demeanor. While Butch seemed to like Susannah instantly, he was thoroughly besotted with Puzzle.

I had only carry-on luggage, so I offered to walk both dogs while Susannah claimed her bags. Puzzle was a consummate professional. Butch, who looks like a giant Muppet come to life, did everything he could to get Puzzle's attention. He bowed, he whimpered, he pawed, but Puzzle remained unmoved by his antics.

It was clear that Puzzle thought she might be on a mission. Every time we passed an official-looking vehicle, she clearly assumed it was there for her and tried to lead me in its direction.

Loading the hotel van with luggage, dogs, and people was chaotic, and through the confusion, Puzzle ended up at my feet. She lay there quietly, seeming almost fragile. As I stroked her back, I felt bump after bump. It took me a moment to figure out that they were the remnants of old wounds—battle scars from her search-and-rescue missions.

Puzzle accepts her abrasions as part of the job she loves. In many ways, Puzzle's work seems more difficult for Susannah, who worries about the physical and emotional stress her dog is constantly under. When they are on a mission, Susannah will hand-feed Puzzle as the dog lies on a soft hotel bed, making every effort to give this hard-working dog a break from her emotional and demanding work.

It is not just the people Puzzle helps to rescue who are indebted to her. It is all of us. Puzzle and dogs like her stand ready and willing to come for anyone who is lost or in need of rescue. Susannah and Puzzle and the work they do clearly illustrate the pure goodness in a dog's heart.

As of last year, most major airlines charge one hundred dollars each way for SAR dogs to fly to rescue missions. *This is insanity.* The vast majority of SAR teams are made up of volunteers who train with their dogs every day and with their teams multiple times a week, all while holding down regular jobs. That these people must pay for their own tickets to disaster zones is sin enough; charging extra to transport these heroic dogs, who take up no more room than a carry-on bag, is reprehensible. I am always proud that Delta is the official airline of Canine Assistants, but never more so than when I learned that they do not charge SAR dogs.

In fact, it was on a Delta flight recently that a woman told me about two lifesaving dogs of a different sort. The woman and her husband had two standard poodles. It was clear that she loved her dogs, and as our conversation progressed, I began to realize the depth of her attachment. She explained, "We had a son named Patrick, our only child, who died of cancer when he was eight."

The woman and her husband had tried for years to have a baby before Patrick was born. She showed me his photograph, taken just before the cancer was diagnosed. As we looked together at the beautiful child, her breathing became deep. "No one tells you how quiet your life, your home, becomes when your only child dies. We got the poodles just to have someone else in the house, someone to look after. We didn't realize how they would bring life back to us, even keep us safe from ourselves." She leaned back into her seat and softly added, "We owe them our lives."

Heroic dogs are everywhere. They work with soldiers, firefighters, SAR personnel, FEMA, and CPB; and with people who have mobility, vision, and hearing impairments, epilepsy, and many other medical and emotional needs. They greet us when we return home each day. They walk beside us when our nights are a dangerous shade of dark, protecting us from threats to our bodies and, at times, to our sanity. They put themselves on the line to deliver us to safety. And they deserve our protection in turn.

CHAPTER SIX

Worldly Dangers

My friend Paula has a highly complex, supersophisticated alarm system in her home, in addition to having four large, relatively vocal golden retrievers. She also has a gun. One day I said, "You are pretty well covered on the safety front with an alarm and dogs for when you're gone, and the dogs and a gun for when you're home."

"Oh, I don't leave the alarm on when I'm gone. I worry about what the police might do if it went off accidentally and my dogs got upset when they came to investigate," she explained. "I have it on when I'm home so that I'd have forewarning and time to get to my dogs if someone broke in to the house."

"I bet it would give a burglar quite a shock, to see those four big dogs coming toward him."

"Toward him?" she exclaimed. "I want time to get them *away* from a bad guy. I have a gun for protection."

I love that woman.

OUR RESPONSIBILITY

It is our responsibility to keep our dogs safe, and not just from bad guys. The world in which our dogs live is full of dangers. Some threats, such as cars and electrical cords, are obvious, while other hazards may come disguised as collars, leashes, and fences, items presumably designed to help keep dogs safe. Whatever the form, dangers lurk, and we must anticipate them, preparing in advance to avoid them.

Bart was a stocky yellow Lab, adopted for training as an assistance dog at eight months of age from a local animal shelter. Although he was obviously intelligent and learned his lessons quickly, he was also what we euphemistically refer to as "a lot of dog." He was so strong and energetic that he tore the door off a cabinet the first time he attempted to tug it open, one of the fundamental tasks of a service dog.

One day I took Bart down to Atlanta to visit the man who sponsored his training. We were driving fifty-five miles per hour on the expressway when suddenly Bart went ballistic, yelping and bouncing all over the car. I later realized a bee had stung him, but at the time, I was solely focused on getting his huge eighty-pound body out from between me and the steering wheel so that I could control the car and see the road. At fifty-five miles per hour, you're traveling 22.5 feet per second, so in the approximately ten seconds it took to get Bart back to his own place, my car had gone more than seventy yards . . . mostly on its own. A great deal can happen on a road in that time and distance. It's no wonder that AAA reports that more than thirty thousand automobile accidents each year are caused by loose pets in the car.

Bart made me an instant believer in restraining dogs in cars. That means not letting your dog ride in your lap and not letting him put his head out the window—two things that, although popular with many dog owners, are fraught with danger. Some people choose to crate their dogs in the car, particularly when driving long distances. Others prefer seat belts or car seats. I am a fan of the latter two. Seat belts, while not perfect, seem to offer the best protection for large dogs, and car seats seem best for smaller dogs, allowing them to still see out the window.

Bart and I, along with the hundreds of other drivers on the road at the time of our incident, were fortunate. He calmed down quickly, and I was able to regain control promptly. After the fact, it seemed a bit like vehicular Russian roulette, something I'd rather not play again.

Sometimes situations don't turn out so well. One of my favorite assistance dogs was killed in a dreadful freak accident that unfortunately occurred in front of the dog's little boy. The big golden had been outside playing with another dog, a black Labrador, when the Lab's muzzle became caught in the golden's martingale collar. The more the Lab twisted and fought to free himself, the tighter the collar became on the golden. By the time the family could release the collar, it was too late.

I knew that it was unsafe to leave metal choke chains, something I detest anyway, on dogs when they are not leashed, but I had given no thought to the fact that the same was true of every other collar that can be twisted enough to cause choking. The only collars safe to leave on your dog when he is off-leash are ones that either break open when pressure is applied or ones that are impossible to twist, such as those made of rolled leather or heavy-duty plastic.

Even if your dog has a microchip, as he should, a collar with identification is a smart idea. At Canine Assistants, we use nylon collars coated with heavy plastic. Each collar has a nameplate riveted on it with our name and phone number. These collars are used for identification purposes only, never attached to a leash, and they remain on at all times. When our dogs are walked on a collar, we use a martingale type that remains affixed to the leash: When the leash comes off, the collar comes off with it.

The leashes we use, except those bolted on to wheelchairs, are all fixed-length or bungee type, rather than the retractable sort incased in hard plastic. Although I appreciate the convenience of a retractable leash, it can cause big trouble for your dog if it slips, as it easily can, out of your hand. Some years ago, a little girl's father was walking one of our assistance dogs, Sabina, on a retractable leash when a car backfired, startling her. The dog jumped, and the dad lost his grip on the leash. As Sabina began to run, the hard plastic casing kept swatting her in the rear, spooking her even more. She was missing for nine days, the longest time any of our dogs has ever been lost. It was the last time we allowed retractable leashes.

The Sabina Incident, as we now refer to it, taught me a great deal about finding lost dogs, even though it took us more than a week to do so. Here is a game plan for finding a lost pet:

1. Start looking immediately. If you don't find your dog within ten minutes, quickly print up some flyers with your dog's photo and your cellphone number. Never use the word *stolen,* even if you saw someone take your dog. You don't want the threat of punishment to prevent someone from returning your dog. Include as large a reward as you can reasonably manage. The reward is often what motivates people to actively search. Rewards can also convince those who have stolen your dog that your dog is worth returning. Note: If someone calls claiming to have your dog, don't hand the money over until you have your dog in your arms. If you must meet the individual somewhere, make certain it is a busy, public place, and take a friend with you.

2. If you can get helpers, come up with a coordinated search plan. Although most people search from their home out, it makes more sense to start at a reasonable perimeter, such as a two-mile radius, and search back toward your house. That way you will likely be ahead of your dog rather than behind him. Leave flyers with everyone you pass. Have each searcher take along a squeaky toy or a box of Milk-Bones (something that can be rattled) to catch your dog's attention. Remember to leave someone at home in case your dog returns on his own.

3. While you are out searching, ask someone else to call nearby veterinary clinics and your local animal control depart-

ment. In many places, the police and firefighters will keep an eye out as well. Also ask your caller to post the information on Facebook and request that local Friends share it.

4. Find your postal carrier as soon possible, and give him the information as well.

5. Put up large posters so that people driving by can easily see them. Include only your dog's photo, the reward amount, and your phone number. The fewer words that must be read by passersby, the better.

6. If twenty-four hours pass with no sign of your dog, place an ad in your local newspaper and begin searching your county shelter in person.

7. If forty-eight hours go by with no sign of your dog, take a day or two off to rest and regroup, then renew the search. Dogs are found days, weeks, months, and even years after being lost.

The Stallworths did everything right when Jake and Lexie, two golden retrievers, ran away from their Birmingham, Alabama, home one day in November. They searched, made flyers, and posted the information on Facebook. Hundreds of people joined the search. On the fifth day of the search, the Stallworths received a call from someone who had seen a golden's body near some train tracks. Mr. Stallworth discovered it was their precious Lexie. She had been hit and killed by a passing train. Instantly, Mr. Stallworth knew that Jake wouldn't be far away. He began searching the area and soon spotted Jake at the bottom of a twenty-five-foot ravine, where he appeared to have been thrown. As he called home for help, Mr. Stallworth slid himself into the ravine with his dog. Jake was alive but seriously hurt. As night fell, firefighters gently removed the injured golden, Mr. Stallworth insisting the dog be taken out first.

Upon admission to the veterinary emergency clinic, Jake was unable to move his back legs. After being stabilized, he underwent a complex spinal surgery to fuse several fractured vertebrae in his back. He made it out of surgery and began the long recovery that would get him home before Christmas. As I write, Jake is able to stand and walk, although his right rear leg is not yet fully functional. The prognosis is good.

Jake and Lexie had escaped an invisible fence before they became lost. I must confess that I am becoming increasingly uneasy about invisible fences for most situations. My sister installed one as a backup to her solid fence in an effort to keep her terrier from escaping the yard through various, often ingenious, methods. The invisible fence, in combination with the solid one, has likely saved the terrier's life. But I have heard a growing number of stories illustrating serious problems associated with invisible fencing, such that I'm no longer comfortable with them.

Even when invisible fences do contain dogs, other problems can occur. One Saturday in December, a police officer in a community south of Atlanta shot and killed a golden retriever in the dog's own yard. The dog, Boomer, was inside a yard enclosed by an invisible fence, but no signs were posted, so the officer was unaware that the dog was "behind a fence." The officer was investigating a suspicious-person sighting in a neighborhood where several burglaries had recently occurred. As he walked past Boomer's yard, the dog jumped off the porch and ran toward the officer, barking. The officer explained that he shouted for the dog to stop, but when the dog did not, he was forced to draw his weapon and shoot. The dog belonged to a fourteen-year-old boy who lives with his widowed mother and five siblings.

I have no doubt that the officer was frightened. Golden retrievers are large, and not everyone knows what to look for or how to respond to seemingly aggressive dogs. Since this incident, I have been asked to train several local police departments on how to react when encountering dogs in the line of duty. Of course the officers cannot risk their own safety, but there are ways of handling these situations (far more common than one might imagine) that stop short of shooting the dog, except in extreme cases.

However, the fence might have contributed to the problem as well, making this highly social dog afraid of people walking past his yard and causing him to bark in a way that could have been construed as aggressive. I imagine the problem began with Boomer's desire to visit with people who were walking down the street. When he tried to do so, he received a shock. He then began associating people passing his yard with pain, and he was forced to bark in an assertive manner to warn people away. The shooting was distressing for everyone involved, but it was Boomer alone who paid with his life.

There are other concerns with invisible fences. Some dogs will run through the shock zone if they feel the pain is worth the reward, such as when in pursuit of a deer or a rabbit or even a ball. Once outside the fence, the dog cannot get back in without being shocked again, and the return might not seem as rewarding. In addition, an invisible fence might keep your dog *in,* but it does not keep other animals *out.* Nor does it prevent your dog from being stolen.

Solid fences are not perfect, either. Gates can be left open, boards can rot, and dogs can dig holes under many barriers. At Canine Assistants, the first rule of the farm is to close *all* doors and gates behind you, even if you plan to be out for only a moment. Our neighbors bolted a sign to their gate as a gentle reminder to those entering their yard:

> PLEASE CLOSE THE GATE SO OUR DOG WILL NOT ROAM.
> WE LOVE HIM SO MUCH AND WE NEED HIM AT HOME!

Come Here

The best possible solution is to always go outside with your dog, or at least keep a close eye on him while he is outside. But if something such as an open gate does present itself while you are there, regaining control of your dog is of utmost importance.

CHOICE TEACHING

Some years ago, I realized that dogs were capable of more than habitual, automatic responses to cues, and that once they understood what was being requested, they could decide for themselves if performing that behavior was in their best interest. It became clear to me that there were two ways to encourage dogs to do what you asked. You could make them *afraid not to* comply through aversive techniques, such as leash corrections and nose thumps; or you could make them *want to* comply by using positive motivation, the latter being infinitely easier, not to mention kinder and gentler.

I do not teach dogs using fear or force. I have repeatedly seen that aversive methods, among other undesirable effects, reduce the rate of learning and have a negative impact on the all-important relationship between a dog and his handler. Conversely, I have seen that dogs who are given the opportunity to comply willingly are quicker to learn a behavior, more eager to work on it, and more likely to repeat it in the future. Understanding this concept led to the development of my Choice Teaching methodology.

In Choice Teaching, a dog is first taught a cued behavior through the use of lures and extrinsic rewards such as treats, toys, and games. Each repetition for which the dog is rewarded creates a positive memory of or association with the behavior in the dog's mind. Once the dog has good feelings about doing as he is asked, subsequent repetitions are intrinsically, or internally, rewarded by the associated positive memories, making extrinsic rewards unnecessary. Here's an example. When teaching a dog to go calmly into a crate, start by tossing treats or kibble into the crate while saying, "Kennel." Over the course of several days, begin encouraging the dog to enter the crate *before* giving him the treat. Ultimately, the act of getting into the crate simply feels good to the dog, and he goes willingly, whether given a reward or not.

Choice Teaching leads to calm, well-mannered dogs who respect their human partners and enjoy doing as asked. What could be better?

Teaching your dog a reliable recall isn't optional; it is a mandatory part of responsible dog guardianship. At Canine Assistants, we use the cue phrase *Come here* for recalls rather than the more common one-word command *Come*. It is easier to make the two-word prompt sound upbeat rather than angry. Pretend that you are in a hurry to get your dog in from the yard, and test the two different cues. "Come" is a short, sharp sound, while "here" lends itself to a high pitch and has a softer feel. Dogs, like people, are far more likely to move toward a friendly and relaxed sound. Anger or tension in your voice might make your dog hesitate. No matter how long it takes him to reach you, always lavish praise on him when he does; it'll encourage him to do it again.

Remember, when your dog can see you, you should turn in the direction you want him to move. If you are facing the direction in which he is headed, he will believe that he's already going the right way and that you will catch up . . . eventually!

When teaching the recall, it's important to ensure that your dog truly knows his name, so begin with a day or two of practice. Put half your dog's daily kibble ration in a bag, storing it in your pocket. Whenever your dog's attention is focused elsewhere, say his name. If he looks at you or orients his body in your direction, smile at him and tell him what a good boy he is as you treat him to some kibble. The smiling, praising, and treating should all be done simultaneously so that each adds value to the others. Repeat this exercise throughout the day. When your dog consistently looks at you or angles toward you when hearing his name, try getting his attention using other names. If he responds to the incorrect call, don't smile, speak, or treat. After a count of three, even if he's still looking at you, say his name, and if he responds appropriately, reward him.

Once you are confident that your dog can understand his name, you are ready to proceed to the next step, the indoor recall. Divide half his daily kibble ration among six different bags. Stash the bags around your house, being careful to put them where there is no chance your dog can reach them by himself. Every time you walk by a stash, call your dog's name and follow that with "Come here." When your dog reaches you, smile, praise, scratch him lightly on the chest, and give him a few pieces of kibble. Eventually, we are going to use praise, smiling, and scratching as stand-alone rewards, so be sure to use them with your food treats initially to help your dog have positive feelings about these reinforcers. Repeat throughout the day. Increase the amount of distraction slowly by having a helper pat him while you call him from another room, having a helper actively play with him in another room while you call him, and, finally, calling him while he is eating from his bowl.

When your dog quickly responds to your indoor recall, move outside to a safely fenced-in area. With half his daily kibble ration tucked into your pocket, let him meander until he becomes engaged by something other than you. As soon as that happens, say his name and "Come here." When he reaches you, smile, praise, scratch him lightly on the chest, and treat him to several pieces of kibble. Slowly increase the distance from which you ask him to recall. When he is easily running across the yard at your cue, begin adding in distractions, as you did on the indoor recall. You can even add an additional dog or two to the yard for guaranteed megadistractions.

Once your dog has amazing recall, stop using kibble as your food reward and replace it with something else your dog absolutely loves. Give him the uber-treat along with the other forms of reward the first three times you recall him. Then, move to using only your smile, praise, and a scratch for two recalls. On the third recall, add the tasty treat back to the mix. Over time, you can move to using the tasty treat on a random basis or about once out of every five to six recalls. It is more exciting for your dog if he never knows when the big reward will come.

If your dog reaches the point that he will not leave your side while you're out together, that's great. But that focus must be reinforced so that it will continue, and we can't use the *Come here* cue since he's already here. So, begin teaching him the cue *Watch me,* meaning, "I want you to make eye contact." Place a treat between your thumb and forefinger and hold it up near your eyes. When your dog makes eye contact (even though he's really just seeing the treat in front of you), smile, praise, and treat. Repeat this process three times. Then put the treat in your pocket and merely tap your finger between your eyes as you say, "Watch me." If he does as asked, reward him with food, a smile, and praise. Repeat three times. Next, try giving your dog only the verbal *Watch me* cue. If he does it, reward with extra treats and the other rewards. If he doesn't, go back to using your finger to merely indicate the spot where he should look. Slowly increase the distance between your finger and face until you feel he is ready to move on to a verbal cue alone. As with the other cued behaviors, use food for the first three times and then randomly.

Freeze

At Canine Assistants, I teach new recipients and volunteers my methodology for living and working with dogs. One particular lesson, which I call Meals for Manners, encourages safety behaviors on cue. In the past, we have used *Come here, Sit,* or *Stay* as emergency commands, but I have found one I prefer to any of these—*Freeze.*

It's a simple cue, meaning "Stop in your tracks," an easier behavior for a dog to perform, when distracted, than "Come here." Consider that in order to "come here," your dog must stop whatever interesting thing he is doing, turn toward you, and move in your direction—three separate and distinct behaviors all chained together. Even *Sit* and *Stay* require that the dog first stop a current activity and second perform an alternative behavior. *Freeze* is a single behavior, "be still." Every dog guardian should teach this behavior and then practice until it's second nature to your dog and he responds 100 percent of the time. This is an all-important safety cue. It's also easy and fun. My son loves working on it with our dogs because there is a little bit of a cops-and-robbers feel to it.

I start by asking someone to stand approximately six feet away from me, holding the dog lightly by the collar. Without saying anything, I toss a treat high in the air toward the middle of the dog's back, about ten or twelve times. (The point of throwing toward the dog's back is to make sure he doesn't have to step forward in order to get the treat, hence the *Freeze* cue.) Once the dog is focused on me, I ask my helper to let go of his collar, and I once again begin tossing the treats, high in the air toward the middle of his back. He has to wait for the treat to come down, yet he doesn't have to move off his spot in order to get it. After approximately six treats, I begin adding the word *Freeze* as I make my underhand throwing motion, just ahead of tossing the treat. Next I begin making the motion of tossing *without* throwing any treats a time or two, before actually pitching one.

Gradually increase the distance from which you ask your dog to "Freeze," and slowly decrease your underarm throwing movement until you have eliminated it altogether, so that your dog is responding only to your spoken cue. If you can't throw the treats far enough to reach your dog from a distance, ask your helper to secretly drop a treat as you make the motion. After you feel certain that your dog understands the word *Freeze,* begin increasing distractions.

Leave It, Take It

Using food as a reward when teaching your dog a new behavior is the best technique for encouraging future repetitions of the behavior, while reinforcing your benevolent leadership. However, it is imperative that your dog learns to "leave it" on cue before you can easily incorporate food rewards into many teaching situations. Having a strong *Leave it* will also help you prevent your dog from grabbing potentially harmful items such as pills, chicken bones, and the brownie in the hand of the toddler next door.

Our teaching techniques evolve as we test and validate new approaches. My latest method for teaching *Leave it* has been used in the dog community for some time, and recent trials at Canine Assistants indicate it's easy to learn and extremely successful. It also has the additional advantage of teaching your dog the meaning of *Take it* in the process. Instructing and proofing *Leave it* can take weeks, so go as slowly as necessary to keep your dog successful at his efforts. Again, as with people, ensuring success is the most important part of any teaching course with dogs.

While your dog is watching, hold a piece of kibble in your hand and make a fist. Place the fist within easy reach of your dog's nose. Allow him to sniff, paw, lick, or whatever he wishes to do to your hand without comment or smile. The second he pauses in his efforts and stops touching you, open your fist, smile, and hold the kibble out for him to eat while saying, "Take it." Repeat this several times, until you are certain your dog understands that his not touching your fist is what gets him the reward. Once he understands this concept, add in the verbal cue *Leave it* as you enfold kibble in your fist, holding it where the dog can reach it. Reward his *Leave it* (not touching your fist) by opening your hand, smiling, and saying, "Take it." After three immediate rewards, make him hold the *Leave it* for a count of three before giving him the *Take it* sequence. After two trials, at a count of three increase your count to five for the third trial, then ten, and then twenty. When he is patient with *Leave it* for a count of twenty while the treat is enclosed in your fist, open your hand so that the reward is visible through the whole process, and repeat your initial sequence, starting with the count of three and working up to a count of twenty.

When you have a dog who reliably performs *Leave it* while you have kibble in your hand, you can move to a piece on the floor. Be very careful through this process because you do not want your dog to grab the food before you can stop him. (Don't panic if he does, however; it just makes it a little more difficult for him to understand right and wrong in this exercise.) Place the kibble on the floor, keeping your hand lightly over it. Give the *Leave it* command, and then reward his compliance by *picking up* the food and performing the *Take it* sequence. You want him to eat kibble from your hand as opposed to the floor, because it sets a good precedent. He is allowed to eat what you give him, not what is on the floor. With each repetition, reduce the proximity of your hand to the kibble and then the length of the time he must "leave it." Do this until you are able to stand upright and ask him to "Leave it" for a long count of twenty. Once again, pick up the food for the *Take it* sequence. Then begin backing away, just one step per repetition, as you ask for the *Leave it*. If he begins to go for the food, make a sharp "ainck" noise (like a honking duck), which should be enough to reinforce the *Leave it*.

Once you have confidence in his willingness to leave a single piece of kibble on the floor when you are twenty steps away, try four or five pieces at once. Start close, and slowly back away. Reward him with only one piece at a time so that he is doing a long, almost automatic *Leave it* with the remaining pieces on the floor.

Finally, start proofing this behavior by using items that are much higher in value to him, such as cheese or squeaky toys. Each time you work with a new item, go back to holding it closed in your hand first, and progress at a rate that keeps your dog successful. Having a good *Leave it* will help you keep your dog safe from many of the dangers in your house, but you still need to perform a thorough evaluation of potential household dangers.

Families who have dogs must dog-proof their homes much as you childproof a house for a toddler. In order to do a good job, you are going to have to get down on your dog's level and take a dog's-eye view of your home. Dogs, not having hands, frequently rely on their mouths to evaluate new objects. Check to be sure that all electrical cords and cables are out of the dog's reach. Be sure that objects small enough to choke your dog are out of the way. Put items such as plastic bags, batteries, and medications in safe places. Once you have finished checking your house, check your garage and your yard. Remember that toys such as tennis balls are extremely dangerous to dogs if you allow them to play unattended. Any toy that your dog could conceivably tear into swallow-sized pieces should be put up when you are not with him. In Appendix B, you will find a list of common household poisons, including poisonous plants, foods, and chemicals, but in general, if you would not want a toddler to chew or ingest something, it probably isn't safe for your dog, either.

CHAPTER SEVEN

Inner Dangers

The outside world is dangerous for your dog. But the inner workings of your dog's mind can be every bit as perilous for him. Growling and putting things in his mouth—such as human skin—are fundamental dog behaviors, but they can prove lethal.

Our expectations of dogs are absurdly high, far higher than our expectations of people. Consider this: How long has it been since you raised your voice in anger or frustration? If someone you didn't know approached you in a manner you considered threatening and trapped you against a wall, would you scream? Lash out? I would probably do both, and no one would blame me in the least. Yet if a dog growls, snaps, or bites, the dog is taken to be fierce, maybe even out of control—unless, of course, the dog is acting in justifiable defense of us, in which case we want our dog to behave like Cujo on steroids.

As part of keeping our dogs safe, we need to understand what dangerous behavior is, causes of it, how to prevent it, and, if prevention isn't possible, how to treat or manage it.

Though I'd always heard about Adopt a Golden Atlanta, I'd not had much personal involvement with them until I began searching online for a dog for my eight-year-old son's BGF (best girlfriend) and her family. This was to be their first family pet, and I wanted to make sure they adopted a dog who would be kind, gentle, and easy. Goldens were an obvious choice.

As I went through the photos of goldens available, my eye was repeatedly drawn to a young male named Winston. He was strikingly handsome, with a large head and a beautiful light coat. Yet something about his wrinkled, worried expression made me want to know more. His bio explained that he was two years old and had been turned in to Adopt a Golden by his family. The reason given was disobedience. It went on to elaborate that he had been sent to an Atlanta trainer who studied under Cesar Millan and that she had used forceful, dominating methods on him for two weeks. Now he needed a home with a strong "alpha" he could not dominate. I was calling the rescue program before even finishing the report. Although Winston was totally wrong for my son's friend and her family, his story was intriguing. I needed to work with him to confirm everything I knew about human-dog relationships, so I set about adopting him.

"I want you to understand that Winston had always been a great dog. My husband feels so betrayed by this whole situation. I am not sure he will ever be able to trust a dog again." Those were the first words I read on the owner-surrender form for Winston, written by the forty-two-year-old wife. I was immediately concerned. Imagine how horrifying the actions of this dog must have been to make a grown man feel "betrayed." I found myself hesitant to read further, but I forced myself through the remainder of the story. I soon realized that it was worse than I could have imagined—for the dog.

The couple, particularly the husband, took dog ownership very seriously. He had read all of Cesar Millan's books and was a faithful viewer of his television show, applying all that he learned to Winston. Although he was generally kind, he felt strongly that his dog needed to be shown that he, the husband, was the boss, the alpha. Otherwise, he feared that the dog would begin to dominate him, and all control would be lost.

One evening, the man was thirty minutes late getting home from work—not usually a big deal, but that night the couple had reservations at a nice restaurant, so both he and his wife were hurried and stressed. Winston was let out into the fenced yard for a quick bathroom break. When Winston didn't return immediately, the man went out to look for him. His wife described his demeanor as irritated. He roughly grabbed Winston's collar and began pulling him into the house. Once inside, he began pushing Winston into his crate. According to his wife, Winston put his mouth on her husband's hand. Her husband then slapped the dog across the muzzle and renewed his efforts to shove him into the crate. Winston then snapped at the man. The husband stood to his full six-foot-two height and kicked the dog across the kitchen floor. When the man went over to the now-cowering dog and reached down to grab his collar, Winston bit him.

Early the next morning, the wife took the dog to the vet's office and demanded that Winston be euthanized because "he had become vicious and unstable." The vet kindly refused and asked for permission to turn the dog over to Adopt a Golden. The husband had required no medical treatment of any sort, not even a Band-Aid. None of the supposedly "vicious" behavior Winston demonstrated had even broken skin.

There are a multitude of classifications for aggression in dogs, depending on what behaviorist you ask, and nearly as many ways to treat or manage the behaviors. There are also a variety of ways to classify dog bites. In the midst of this muddle, there is one thing of which I am certain: *Reacting to a dog's aggression with aggression of your own does not work and, in many cases, makes things significantly worse.*

Placing Winston with a trainer who was an aggressive dominance theorist made him more afraid of people and considerably more likely to lash out. The dangerous aspect of many of these methods is that the trainers, who use harsh punishments, are rarely the people who get bitten. The dogs are usually too afraid to react much, except in an effort to appease them. Some years ago, I asked a psychologist friend of mine, who'd done research on the effects of abuse on behavior in dogs and children, why she thought some dogs looked so happy while under the care of mean or aggressive individuals. I hoped she would say that the treatment could not be that terrible if the dogs still seemed happy. That isn't what she said. People and dogs learn to do all in their power to appease their abuser, she explained. Artificial good cheer is a very common form of appeasement, a component of traumatic bonding.

Traumatic bonding, as psychologist Donald Dutton labeled it, is the behavior produced when affection and violence are combined. Studies done on dog behavior reveal that dogs appear more bonded to trainers who alternately abuse and reward them. The affection does just enough to keep hope alive. Much like what happens in cases of human domestic abuse, the victim begins to believe that if they are just "good enough," everything will be okay. Imagine what that must look, and feel, like in a dog's mind. Dogs treated in this manner must remain hypervigilant in order to avoid "deserving" punishment. Good behavior in these relationships isn't based on affection and understanding. It is based on terror.

It is only when the dog begins having a relationship with an owner who is kind 99 percent of the time that trouble starts. The dog begins to slowly relax, believing that the person will not harm him. As the terror begins to fade, so does the hypervigilance. Then something, such as Winston's failure to come in from the yard when the man called, triggers a change in the relationship. The man, believing the "experts" on television, thinks that Winston deliberately disobeyed. The man, in an effort to establish his dominance, and feeling righteous indignation, lashes out to show the dog who is boss. Winston, who probably just wanted to sniff one last grassy spot or smell the evening air, had no idea that his owner believed he was staging a coup, attempting to take control of the house. From Winston's point of view, the man had suddenly and unpredictably become dangerous. When the man behaved aggressively, with no forewarning or discernible reason, Winston, for once in his life, defended himself. For this, he lost his home and very nearly his life.

Fighting back should, in fact, be considered much healthier than passively absorbing abuse. After all, some degree of aggression is a necessary part of any species's survival. In truth, Winston showed remarkable restraint. First, he took the man's hand in his mouth, exerting no pressure. And even after being slapped, shoved, and kicked across the room, he bit without causing injury. Although I'm not suggesting that any trainer on television or otherwise would recommend kicking a dog across a room, the dominance model seems to give dog owners the express permission to do what's necessary to establish who is the boss.

Very few rescue organizations in the country would have taken Winston. Almost all rescue groups refuse to accept dogs who have displayed aggression toward humans or other animals. Although I realize that there are many dogs in need, excluding every dog accused of aggression regardless of mitigating factors seems a dreadfully shortsighted way to determine which dogs live and which dogs die.

When I was a little girl, my neighbors, the Hastings family, had three children with whom I played: two girls, who were close to my own age, and one boy, who was a few years younger.

One day I was in the kitchen making cookies with Mrs. Hastings and one of the girls when the little boy came in sobbing with blood running down his cheek. "Buddy bit me!" he cried. "*What* did you do to that poor dog?" was Mrs. Hastings's immediate reply.

The Hastingses were not particularly dog people. They never had one of their own while I knew them. Still, Mrs. Hastings knew that Buddy, a yellow Lab who lived next door, was a friendly sort and never outside his fenced yard without his owners. She correctly assumed that any blame in this incident would fall squarely on the shoulders of her son, who had no business being in the neighbors' backyard or messing with their dog without permission. Moments later, the neighbors returned the little boy's lasso, which they had found wrapped around Buddy's back legs.

The little boy's wound was really more of a cut than a bite and didn't require any stitches. The Hastingses certainly weren't mad at Buddy and even forced the child to apologize to the dog for using him as a make-believe calf for roping. The dog gave the child multiple kisses of forgiveness. As the Hastingses and I walked back to their house, the little boy said, "He wasn't much of a cow, anyway."

At some point between then and now, we stopped taking responsibility for our own actions and those of our children and began demanding kind, submissive behavior from dogs regardless of the circumstances. It's time we reevaluate our expectations. In most states, if a child runs onto your property and hits your dog repeatedly with a stick, your dog is expected to take the abuse without issuing so much as a nip in correction.

In some counties, there is a "one and done" law, requiring that any dog who bites (or even breaks the skin of a human with a scratch) be destroyed. Not long ago, an Atlanta-based rescue organization fought to get a golden out of a shelter in Florida before he was euthanized. The dog's owner had him on a leash and was standing in her own driveway when a neighbor child ran up to the dog and threw a stick at the dog's feet. Dog and child bent down to retrieve the stick at the same time, and the child came up with a very shallow puncture wound from the dog's tooth. It was obviously an accident, but the child's parents called the animal control authorities, who came and took the dog to the pound to be quarantined. Because this was a "one and done" county, the dog's owners frantically tried to save him. The rescue group agreed to transport the dog out of state the moment he was released from quarantine. The request was denied, and the county euthanized a happy, friendly golden retriever.

Having such unrealistic societal expectations of canine behavior is every bit as abusive as puppy mills and dog fighting.

Parents, *do not* let your children approach unfamiliar dogs without permission. Teach them not to put their faces in a dog's face. Explain that dogs can bite when frightened. In presentations, I often ask people to tell me the proper way to approach an unfamiliar dog. The answer is, *never* approach an unfamiliar dog. Tell your children that if a dog wishes to interact, he should be allowed to come to you. Explain that a wagging tail and a smiling face are not necessarily signs that a dog wants to be petted. Many children mistake a snarl for a smile in a dog.

Clarify that when an owner says you may pet a dog, you should cup your hand and scratch under his chin. Tell kids never to reach over a dog and pat him on the head, because the dog might misinterpret the intent, thinking you are going to hit him. Children should be told to never try riding a dog, no matter how big he is. They should also know not to pull on any part of a dog.

Children should learn never to run from dogs, because running will make dogs chase them. When a dog runs toward a child, the child should stand still, give himself a hug to keep his hands still, and lean over a bit so the dog isn't encouraged to jump up on the child. Then, he should look down so that he isn't looking at the dog, something that may encourage a dog to interact in some manner. Most dogs are playful with children, but if the dog knocks a child down and causes an injury, that counts as a "dog bite." So, for the sake of both children and dogs, education is critical.

Since working with rescue organizations, I've come to realize another distressing reality. Owners are not totally forthcoming about their dogs when giving them up to rescue. My assumption: No owner would want to disclose anything bad about his dog. He wouldn't admit that his dog had bitten someone or committed any other such atrocity. And I'm sure that deception happens. But it is the owners who falsely exaggerate their dogs' aggressive tendencies who astonish me. It seems that people feel compelled to present what they perceive as an acceptable reason for giving a dog away. If they said, "I hit the dog and he growled at me," then giving the dog up would not be okay, so they say the dog went after them for no reason. Better that the dog be destroyed as irreparably vicious than that they be embarrassed.

Consequently, not all owner-reported aggression should automatically be accepted as fact. Owners simply might not tell the truth, or they might be trying to tell the truth but have seriously misinterpreted the situation. Not all aggression is intended to be threatening. Sometimes a growl is merely a dog's way of telling you he is uncomfortable. I appreciate it when a dog growls at me. It is a form of ritualized aggression that allows me time to change my behavior or the situation before getting bitten.

There is a tremendous difference between *ritualized* aggression and *true* aggression. True aggression in dogs—in any species—is so rare as to be nearly statistically nonexistent. It isn't biologically advantageous. True aggression of the no-holding-back, I'm-coming-at-you-with-all-I-have, consequences-be-damned variety, is extremely costly to the participants, both physically and emotionally. The cost, often a life, is too risky for the benefit received.

On the other hand, all species display ritualized aggression so that realistic outcomes can be decided without anyone having to die. People play football, have shouting matches or fistfights, or sue one another as a form of ritualized aggression. Dogs have their own forms, such as growling, snarling, snapping, and biting with minimal force. It is only when we two species, dogs and humans, believe that the other is out to kill, and meet aggression with aggression, that we get ourselves into trouble.

KINDER, GENTLER

Adopt a Golden Atlanta no longer uses trainers who subscribe to the alpha model or use aversive training methods such as shock collars. Currently, dogs who have gotten into significant trouble first come to me so that I can design a plan for their rehabilitation or management. Adopt a Golden Atlanta is a large, well-respected rescue organization, and because they carry the banner of positive reinforcement, others will surely follow. I'm pleased and proud of the commitment they've made. They would have found their own way toward a more positive training method eventually, but I like to believe that the change in philosophy came about largely thanks to Winston—or Hudson, as he is now known.

The first thing I do with adopted dogs is change their names, so Winston became Hudson. Names can develop negative connotations for dogs, and I want to give them a fresh start. Hudson is still looking for his forever home, but for now, he is happy at Canine Assistants. The one and only time Hudson has shown any aggression while here was when I was stupidly, jokingly fussing at another dog for getting into the trash just as I reached to grab Hudson's collar. He snarled and snapped at me as he simultaneously urinated on the floor. He isn't mean; he's afraid.

This case has had a profound impact on me. I knew theoretically that there were many dogs such as Hudson, and virtually all rescue programs are reporting an increase in the number of biters being surrendered by their owners. But this was the first time that I looked into the eyes of a dog who had come so close to being euthanized due solely to human stupidity.

RESOURCE GUARDING

How can we keep our dogs safe from their own natural dog behaviors? It is important that they understand and meet human expectations; helping them practice, internalize, and enjoy behaving in ways that people find acceptable dramatically lessens the risk of objectionable behaviors.

Possession is 100 percent of the law in their world. If a dog has an item and truly wants to keep it, it is socially unacceptable for another to take that item away. This has nothing to do with dominance. The law is equally applicable to dogs of all ages and social positions. An adult dog will not try to take a bone away from a puppy. The rule of canine law is clear and generally well followed.

Sharing goes against instinct for most dogs but can be easily taught. At Canine Assistants, we use a simple quid-pro-quo method. As noted earlier, once your dog has learned *Leave it* and *Take it,* ask him to take an item of high value, such as a rawhide bone. While he is engaged with the bone, get a treat of equal (or higher) value, approach your dog with a smile, and pleasantly say, "Mine, please," while taking the bone back with one hand and luring your dog's nose toward the delicious treat with the other. Allow him to eat the treat. While holding his collar, hand the bone back to him, smiling and saying, "Take it."

Be cautious, as this giving up of goods in his possession does not come naturally to a dog. If he goes still, snarls, growls, or in any other way seems unhappy about your approaching him while he is with his bone, back away immediately. *Do not insist.* He isn't trying to dominate you, but he *is* uncomfortable, and pushing the situation might get you bitten and your dog in trouble. If he handles the exchange without a problem, make practicing it a common exercise to prevent the development of resource guarding.

Also, it is sensible to do exercises designed to prevent food aggression in your dog. Begin by asking your dog if he wants his dinner. Pretend to his prepare food as usual, but, instead of putting the food in his regular bowl, place it, along with several of his favorite treats, in another, making sure the bowl containing the food isn't visible to him. Next, set the dog's empty bowl on the floor. When your dog realizes that there is no food in it, he will look up at you as if to say, "Hey! What gives?" When he does, pick up the empty bowl and put a very small amount of regular food (just a few pieces of kibble) in it from his hidden meal. Repeat this several times. Now pick up the bowl, put only two of the treats in it, and return it to the floor. Once he has eaten those, place the remainder of the meal in his bowl, and while he is eating it, ask if he wants a treat, dropping one into his bowl. Finally, if you feel completely safe, pick up his bowl as he is eating, drop the remaining treats on top of the kibble, and place it back on the floor.

When your dog learns that picking up his bowl means something positive, the addition of delicious treats, ask other members of your household to do this exercise as well. At every meal, someone should pick up the dog's bowl to add an extra delectable treat. One of the kindest things you can do for your dog is help him understand that people around his bowl at mealtimes is positive; he does not need to feel protective.

Many resource guarders also demonstrate "body guarding," an unwillingness to be touched in a particular manner or spot. When dealing with body guarders, be sure you rule out physical pain as a cause before attempting to modify the behavior.

At Canine Assistants, we recently tested a dog from a local shelter that we were considering for adoption. He was a sweet poodle-retriever mix named Roy, with a large head and a thin, long body. Roy's initial testing as a service dog was outstanding: He knew his basic commands and had a great penchant for retrieving, a necessary aptitude. From afar Roy seemed comfortable, but when I moved to stroke his back, he began a low, throaty growl. I had not yet touched him, and it was clear he did not want me to. He was body guarding. This was the result of having been abused, being in physical pain, or fear of the potential for pain. As it turned out, according to his previous owners, Roy had been injured when jumping off a small wall in their backyard. Ever since then, he would not let anyone touch his back, even though it had long ago healed and was no longer painful. It took months to overcome his guarding, but with the caution, patience, and persistence of his trainers, Roy did, and he loves to have his back rubbed by the family with whom he now lives.

For some dogs, it is too late to prevent resource guarding. But the display of aggression that often goes with this behavior can be lethal, so it must be treated, or at least managed, if your dog is to live safely in the human world. Some pet owners believe that dogs should surrender whatever they might have immediately, upon a simple cue from us, without having been taught the benefits of so doing. In such cases, conflict is inevitable and must be quickly resolved. It is potentially dangerous, especially for children, to live with resource guarders. It is also dangerous for the dogs. Too often, they become aggressive while resource guarding and consequently end up euthanized, being perceived as vicious.

Managing a dog who resource guards is accomplished by removing coveted items from his environment or avoiding confrontation when the dog is guarding an object or location. For dogs who have a history of inadequate food sources—for example, strays found significantly underweight—providing copious amounts of food in a variety of places can be a successful management technique. If the guarded object is dangerous to the dog or necessary to you, offer the dog an irresistible, especially delicious treat in trade. This technique lures him into giving up the item in order to gain access to something better.

Trading works well to manage dogs that resource guard, but it is not going to stop the underlying behavior. For treatment of potentially dangerous resource guarding, the help of an expert may be necessary. It is an owner's decision whether to simply manage resource guarding or treat its root cause. When deciding which path to take, several questions must be considered.

What threat does the dog first use when resource guarding?
Most dogs who resource guard use a series of escalating threats, or
ritualized aggression, such as growling, barking frantically, raising
their hackles, or baring their teeth in a menacing manner. A dog
who begins with a curled lip is much easier to handle than a dog
who starts by chasing you across the kitchen floor.

How many items or locations does he guard? If a dog gets
upset only when he is approached while eating his kibble, leaving
him alone at mealtime may be the only management tool needed. If
he guards multiple items such as toys, food, and his body, you may
need professional help.

**Finally, how vulnerable are the people or animals with
whom the dog has contact?** In an adults-only household,
do-it-yourself management may work fine. However, if there are
small children in the house, even as occasional visitors, seek professional help. If you have another pet who is elderly or frail, you
should also get professional help. Remember, your dog needs you to
keep him safe, so if you have any doubts regarding your ability,
please let someone with expertise in behavioral issues help
you . . . and your dog.

If you want to try treating your dog's mild resource guarding
yourself, Appendix C lays out a sample treatment schedule for one
of the most common behavioral issues, food-bowl guarding. This
method can be modified to treat other resource-guarding issues. But
do not attempt it if you do not feel it is safe for you *or* your dog. I
would not want you to get bitten, and I would not want your dog
to feel as if he must bite. Get professional help if you have any hesitation or concern for your safety.

FINDING A METHOD AND AN EXPERT

People often ask which approach to dog training and management
is best. There are many divergent opinions in the dog world. Although some differences are merely preferences and largely irrele-

vant, others indicate entirely different belief systems about dogs. In determining which approach makes the most sense, you have to ask only one question: Which does science support? Investigate the opinions of the scientists, animal behaviorists, and D.V.M.'s who have spent their careers studying animals and appropriate training and management methods. The websites of programs such as the Family Dog Project and the American Veterinary Society of Animal Behavior are excellent resources. Science might stop short of telling us all we need to know, but it will no longer lead us in the wrong direction.

When searching for a trainer, begin by identifying the ones who use dog-friendly methods of training. Certified members of the Association of Pet Dog Trainers, those who have been accredited through the Certification Council for Professional Dog Trainers, are generally an excellent place to start. Dismiss any trainer who pronounces the need for humans to dominate dogs. These people might have good intentions, but they are dangerously ignorant of what science, and good sense, have taught us about dog behavior. Likewise, any trainer who uses choke chains, pinch collars, or e-collars (shock collars) should be avoided. Plenty of trainers are knowledgeable and talented enough to teach dogs without having to hurt or frighten them. Finally, look for someone who would be willing, even eager, to go with you and your dog to visit a veterinary behaviorist if traditional training approaches are not proving effective. Knowing when to ask for help is important in any field.

COLLAR SENSITIVITY

Because of when and how we use their collars, dogs should undergo collar-desensitization training. Since it's generally true that we grab collars when we are upset or angry or wish to put a stop to playtime, is it any wonder our dogs don't like to be seized by the collar? Some dogs become so uncomfortable that they will use their mouths in an effort to intercept the arm reaching for them. Because most people interpret a dog putting his mouth on human skin as a bite, and because some dogs do not have a good idea of how much pressure to apply for adequate restraint, we must teach our dogs that someone reaching for their collars is not a bad thing.

Start by breaking special treats into pieces smaller than a pencil eraser, and add them to the kibble bags that you've hidden throughout the house (as in the *Come here* exercise described earlier). At various times during the day, call your dog to "come here," and reward him with kibble, not the special treats, for complying. Then reach slowly and gently under his chin, giving him a short, pleasant scratch. When he accepts this attention, smile, praise him, and feed him one of the treat pieces. With each repetition of this process, you should move closer to grabbing his collar from under his chin. For dogs who have not shown any particular sensitivity to the process, you should be able to grab his collar within six attempts. For dogs who do show sensitivity, go slowly. It might take twelve or more repetitions before you feel comfortable grabbing his collar underneath his chin. No matter how long it takes, there are a few points to keep in mind. The first collar grab should be very gentle and only underneath his chin. After he willingly allows this first collar grab, you should praise him enthusiastically and give him several pieces of the yummy treats.

Once you have mastered the under-the-chin collar grab, repeat the process, but this time, reach for the collar on top of his neck. Moving your hand over his head might be more frightening for him; therefore it might take many repetitions over the course of days before you (and he) are comfortable with this grab. Go as slowly as needed. If he acts fearful of your hand, back up to the last point where he accepted your touch without reaction, and progress more slowly. Remember, for rescued or older dogs, you might be undoing years of damage, so patience is critical.

Once your dog accepts gentle collar grabs, begin seizing more quickly, and put more pressure on the collar. Always reward him for allowing your grabs with your smile, kind words, and special treats.

Finally, begin reaching out to grab his collar at random times and in unexpected situations. Again, slowly increase the speed at which you grab and the pressure you exert. Once he shows no negative reaction to having his collar suddenly and forcefully grabbed, you may begin rewarding him with treats on a random basis.

At this point, also begin attaching his leash when he is playing outside in a safely fenced area. Do three or four collar grabs, complete with leash attachments, holding the dog for a few seconds before unsnapping the leash and commanding the dog to "go play." Do not do this initially when you are going inside or stopping the play, to avoid a negative association.

Once your dog has a positive conditioned emotional response (pCER) to having his collar grabbed, you've taken a significant step in ensuring his safety and yours. It is a teaching process that will work with any dog, whether from a shelter or a breeder, who seems uncomfortable with or aggressive toward a collar and leash.

BITES

Dog bites, seen as the pinnacle of aggression, have become an extremely emotional topic in the past few years. Various newspaper articles and websites have warned about the increase in the annual number of bites. According to the reports, it seems no one is safe with any dog, even our beloved family pet. The information provided from the majority of these sources is scary, confusing, and disconcerting—but is it accurate?

Although there are more dog bites now than twenty years ago, there are clear reasons. In today's culture, dogs live inside more often, and the average dog has contact with many more people than the dogs of past generations. In addition, we aren't always nice to our dogs. Today's dominance culture has without doubt frightened many otherwise peaceful dogs into biting.

But, undeniably, dogs have always bitten people, playfully or otherwise. Dogs use their mouths like we use our hands. Oddly, it is only in recent years that we have begun to panic about this. We must rationally consider and assess the entire issue before continuing to ban breeds and label pets as a serious hazard to our health and well-being.

So, how many dog bites occur annually in the United States? An estimate, based on an extremely small sample by the Centers for Disease Control, found that in 2001 there were eight million dog bites or bite-related injuries in the United States. Although this is a startlingly large number, it's difficult to take it seriously, given that there were no criteria regarding the severity or intent of the reported bites. It's conceivable that a majority of those bites were from puppies, something we call "play bites." Several years ago, I fell down the stairs at a friend's house because her six-week-old puppy was nibbling on my shoelaces. The fall resulted in a minor injury that could have been listed as "dog-bite related." So, in the end, eight million reported dog bites is a huge number that just doesn't mean much.

Instead of analyzing vague statistics, let's evaluate the number of dog-bite–related injuries seen in hospital emergency departments. In the same 2001, approximately 370,000 people were seen in emergency rooms for dog-bite–related injuries, and of those, only 1.6 percent were considered serious, with sixteen fatalities. Although these numbers might seem scary, they should be viewed in the context of more than seventy million pet dogs. Given that nearly all dogs, even small ones, walk around with a mouth full of teeth capable of ripping human flesh, it's surprising that there are not more injuries requiring a trip to the local hospital.

Many people believe that banning certain breeds will reduce the risk of dog aggression toward people. It will not. There is no such thing as a bad breed. Pit bulls used to be among the top choices for families with children. It's true that large dogs have big teeth and strong jaws, which make them more dangerous if they do bite, but it does not make them more likely to bite. Although specific breeding can create a dog who is more apt to bite than the average dog, it takes a good deal of constant abuse to raise one willing to do serious harm to a human being. Their evolutionary course is working against this concept. Aggression toward humans is the one trait that has been naturally and artificially selected against for dogs' entire history. It takes careful and intentional breeding, combined with torture, to create a rage greater than restraint in most dogs. Although this could be done with virtually any breed, some, such as Cavalier King Charles spaniels, would take longer than others to reach a breaking point. If a breed ban eliminates pit bulls, rottweilers, Dobermans, and German shepherds, then some depraved individual will begin working on Labradors. Breed bans will never work. People cause the problem, not dogs.

Dogs are inherently safe creatures. You are far less likely to be harmed by a dog than by another human. Still, it's important to make efforts to reduce the number of dog-related injuries, and that can and should be done through the education of both dogs and people. Consider that the majority of bites involving small children are to the face. Therefore, children must be taught the importance of not engaging a dog in a manner that might result in a facial bite, such as face-to-face or nose-to-nose play. If the child is too young to understand this concept, keep dogs and children separated when not being closely supervised. Remember that if a small child's behavior is likely to irritate another child, it is likely to irritate a dog.

What if someone, about your size or larger, came running toward you screaming and moving in an odd, unpredictable manner—just as hundreds of thousands of parents allow their children to do to unfamiliar dogs every single day? Can we honestly say that dogs are to blame in these situations?

Although it might not be fair, we do place blame on our dogs. Last night, a veterinarian told a group of us studying aggression about a young dog that had bitten a toddler in the face for what the owners believed was absolutely "no reason." Although the child was not badly injured, the parents, assuming the bite was unprovoked, insisted that the dog be euthanized. After the dog was put to sleep, a postmortem examination revealed that a small pencil had been jammed into the dog's ear, perforating his eardrum and undoubtedly causing terrible pain.

Dogs cannot push children away with their hands or speak the words *Leave me alone*. The only true protection they have is their teeth—and fear and misunderstanding are the principal reasons they end up using them. If those uncertainties can be negated, the possibility that a dog will bite is substantially reduced. We must teach our dogs bite inhibition so that, if they do bite human skin, they will not bite down hard. In Appendix D, you will find a guide to teaching adult dogs how to have gentle mouths.

Dogs rely on our protection. They have no one else. We must socialize them, teach them bite inhibition, and keep them out of situations, such as being left alone with a young child, where they might do unintended harm. We must demonstrate that humans are trustworthy companions, and honor that trust in all that we do. We should use our brilliant human brains, taking responsibility for those who need us, and realize that dogs are dogs—sometimes they have to growl, snap, and even bite. Most important, we must move past the notion that dogs and humans are somehow adversaries and that we must dominate them before they dominate us. It's a concept that is killing our dogs.

CHAPTER EIGHT

Teaming Up

Earnest is the first word that came to mind when I met eight-year-old Alexander. As I knelt to ask this little boy what he most wanted his Canine Assistants seizure-response dog to do for him, his big brown eyes narrowed in concentration. He wanted to explain everything clearly and in detail. "You see," he said with great seriousness, "I get picked last for teams . . . if they pick me at all." Although he continued to elaborate, he needn't have bothered. That one sentence explained it all.

Buckley, the first dog Alexander met in our matching process, was a golden retriever who instantly claimed the little boy for himself. After three days of working together, we nicknamed them Team A-B, as the pair already functioned in such perfect harmony it was difficult to see where the child stopped and the dog began.

Just after graduation, a reporter from our local newspaper asked Alexander, "What is the best part of having Buckley?" Alexander replied immediately. "Buckley picked me for his team." He ruffled the big golden's fur, then turned to me and added softly, "Everybody needs a team."

• • •

Not long after Alexander and Buckley graduated, I saw another remarkable example of the power of a human-canine team.

Pop, the Labrador puppy, had never been off the sixteen-acre South Carolina farm where he was born. As a matter of fact, he had rarely left his kennel. The breeders were watching as he matured to see if they wanted to keep him as a stud dog. When Pop's permanent teeth started coming in crooked, they realized he would not be the perfect sire material they'd hoped for. When Pop was six months old, his breeders donated him to Canine Assistants.

As one of our staff members, prone to malapropisms, once said, "Pop was a jumble of nerves." The poor dog seemed afraid of nearly everything. Pop taught me an important lesson about the need for early socialization. Watching him, I realized that many of the dogs who seemed as if they had been physically abused were in fact the victims of accidental sensory deprivation. Living in a kennel, Pop never saw the outside world, or the inside world, for that matter. He was fine with lawn mowers and leaf blowers, but bicycles, hair dryers, and toilets terrified him.

We kept Pop at Canine Assistants for nearly a year, hoping that we could help him acclimate to life outside the kennel before placing him in a pet home. Clearly, he would never function as a companion or service dog. Fortunately, we neglected to mention our reservations to him. Pop went on to be the canine part of one of the strongest assistance-dog teams I've ever seen. The way it happened was a total fluke.

Paul, a seven-year-old boy with Angelman syndrome, had come to one of our two-week training camps to be matched with a helper dog. The first day did not go well. Every dog we introduced to Paul seemed afraid of his outgoing, hug-me-now personality, which is characteristic of Angelman kids. The staff was concerned that we wouldn't be able to find the right dog. As I was expressing my apprehension to Paul and his family, a trainer happened to walk through the office with Pop in tow. In that instant, Pop looked at Paul, immediately pulled away from his trainer, and climbed into the boy's lap. Paul started laughing, and the dog started chuffing. From the second they met, Paul and Pop were made to be together, and that connection allowed Pop to be brave, or at least brave enough.

Ten days later, just before the team's graduation, I was talking to Paul's dad about the dramatic transformation in both Pop and Paul once they met. He explained, "They're good teammates, and everybody needs a team."

"So I've recently been told," I said.

It is not always easy to put into words how much it can mean to have a dog by your side, but one of our Canine Assistants recipients did a beautiful job in a letter she wrote to the people who sponsored her dog.

To everyone who played a part in making Eddie into the gift that he is:

How do I say thank you for a gift like this? How do I find the words to express my gratitude and awe to all of you that have given your time, your hearts, and your money to ease my suffering—someone you don't even know?

I'm Leann, I'm 44 years old and I've had seizures all my life. Everything I do and everything I try to accomplish is affected by my seizure condition.

It has made my life challenging, physically, mentally, and emotionally, but I've had an incredible family and group of friends that have helped me to stay positive and hopeful that things will get better. Even though I know I must never give up, it is often a very hard thing to do. Sometimes I pray for courage, or the strength to persevere. Sometimes, I make desperate pleas or bargains, wondering if I will live through the seizure event. And sometimes, when the seizures come in the middle of the night and I'm awakened into a whirlwind of dread, I am lost and cannot find the strength of will to reach out in prayer for anything at all.

Last night I had a seizure like that. I awoke right in the middle of it. My head was buzzing as if hundreds of bees were lifting away my skull. My stomach lurched and went sour. My body was shaking and for a long time I couldn't speak. I was trapped inside, staring out into the darkness of the room, really scared. My limbs went cold. I had to just wait it out. Time passed slowly. Then, as a thin slice of morning light slipped into the room, my brain finally released me. My eyes began to focus on the calm, steady face lying across from me in the bed. It was Eddie, my service dog from Canine Assistants. He had been lying beside me the whole time. His eyes were quiet, staring into mine. His breath came in soft, short chortles that soothed me. I stared at him for a long moment, listening to his breath and realized that I was clinging to him. My right hand was gripping his ample rolls of extra fur and my left hand was clutching his collar. I took a deep breath and relaxed my grip but he made no movement to pull away or leave me.

Tentatively I reached out and stroked his silky ear and he responded by moving his head closer to mine on the pillow and closing his eyes contentedly. Placing my hand on his chest I began to weep and a very deep, very old prayer rose to my lips. "Thank you," I whispered. "Thank you."

People might ask how can a service dog change one's life? Now, I see it is like asking how kindness and compassion might touch a soul.

Thank you all for being extraordinary and so very generous with your hearts. Thank you for giving me Eddie, who has re-awakened the light in my own heart.

Life is too difficult at times to be lived alone. We all need a team. In order to live a good life, every sentient being needs to belong somewhere and to have the affection of someone who will always be on his side, regardless of the circumstances. A team is far stronger than just the sum of its parts. Among the many blessings dogs give to humankind, none can be greater than the fact that dogs are team players, and miraculously, many have chosen to play on our team.

The team analogy fits perfectly the relationship we share with our dogs. Since coming to appreciate that concept, I've spent a good deal of time talking to people about their views on teams and what it means to be a teammate. My favorite response came from my son's football coach, who said, "Above all, a true teammate is not forgotten and never let go."

I am struck by the realization that dogs often make better teammates for us than we do for them. It seems that people have a tendency to abandon our canine teammates when they struggle. I have seen this repeatedly in my work with rescue programs. I've never seen a dog abandon someone because that person got grumpy, injured, or sick, but I've seen the reverse many times.

Some might suggest that dogs are faithful because they are pack animals and they see us as part of their pack. I disagree. There is increasing evidence that dogs are not pack animals at all. Feral dogs do not form packs. They might form associations, even friendships, but they do not form stable groups resembling true packs. This makes sense when you consider that dogs, even though they are a subspecies of wolves, would not exist were it not for the presence of human beings.

Approximately 135,000 years ago, humans invented the bow and arrow, and as a result, food became more plentiful. This increase in an available food supply created an evolutionary opportunity for any animal brave enough to venture near people and eat the discarded scraps. The wolves who took advantage of this new food source, leaving the wild to risk being close to humans, reproduced among themselves. And, with each generation, the behavior of these pre-dogs became less similar to that of pack-hunting wolves. Physically they remained much the same; their wolf bodies were already beautifully adapted to traveling along with nomadic humans.

It wasn't until approxomately 12,000 years ago that the domestic dog as we know him came into existence. It was then that human beings began using agriculture as their primary food source. Because humans no longer had to roam in order to hunt and gather, they built permanent settlements. These settlements also meant the end of roaming for the predogs who followed humans. The bodies of these animals quickly adapted to more stable living conditions, undergoing noticeable skeletal changes. Man's best friend was born.

Chances are dogs weren't used for hunting until more modern times, because the dogs that lived near humans were scavengers, not hunters. Hunting together and in coordination is a large part of what defines a pack. Modern dogs are not designed to be pack animals; they are designed to be highly social and near people.

Still, dogs are the descendants of wolves, albeit scavenging wolves rather than hunting wolves. As a part of their evolutionary process, dogs began to resemble juvenile wolves, not adult wolves. Although some breeds, such as the pug, are a great deal younger on the wolf-maturation scale than are, say, Alaskan huskies, no dog ever grows up to be just like an adult wolf. Our dogs stay pups forever.

In the wolf family, the breeding male and female, as well as older siblings, work together to nurture a pup. If food is in short supply, it is most likely that the pup, as the youngest, will be allowed to eat before his older brothers and sisters so that his young body can continue developing normally.

It is interesting to note that if a wolf pup grows to adulthood, he will almost certainly become an alpha, but not because he is the biggest and strongest of his siblings and able to dominate those around him. Rather, strength and size have little to do with becoming an alpha. Virtually all wolves become alphas if they endure long enough to reproduce, because *alpha* simply means the parents in a pack. Other than its possible influence on survival in harsh conditions, machismo is not a factor.

It is fascinating how misunderstood the concept of *alpha* has become in our society. *Alpha male* has effectively replaced *macho man* in our lexicon. But it is horrifying to consider how much damage this misunderstanding has caused, and this isn't solely a dangerous trend for our dogs. The acceptability of mistreatment in a society tends to move from animals to children to women. Note this example from an article entitled "Teach Your Child Like You Train

Your Dog" by Brenda Nelson on Gomestic.com, a new parent website:

> In the dog world a dog who runs the house is called the Alpha Dog. It is generally frowned on for the owner to allow their dog to be the boss of the house. When we look at some families we can see a five-year-old human child has become the Alpha.
>
> Parents often feel guilty about confining their baby or toddler in a playpen, yet if introduced to them correctly young children can play in a confined space safely for a short period of time. The trick is to introduce them to the playpen at a young age and to leave them in it for a little while, removing them when they are good. If you remove them when they are fussing you reward them for fussing, much like you reward a puppy for crying if you take it out of the crate too soon.
>
> Sound cruel? Think of adults who work in cubicles. Everyone has to learn somewhere.

Perhaps even more troubling was one reader's comment on the article:

> I totally agree with you, you know what they say, "You have to be cruel to be kind."

This is from an article entitled "Secrets to Becoming the Alpha Male" by James Brito that I found on eioba.com, a site that allows people to self-publish articles, many of them in the "how to" category:

> When a girl, particularly one you've just met at a bar or any social venue, treats you with disrespect, it's up to you, as the "alpha male," to ignore her. Shut her out, move on, and she'll eventually come back to you the same way a dog would: with her tail between her legs, apologetic, and hungry for your re-

spect. But don't address her until you're sure you have her re-spect, otherwise you're allowing her to "move up in the pack," which, as with dogs, will only create future problems.

You can even apply the alpha dog training to dates. Since the alpha leader eats first, chooses what to eat, and eats the big-gest portions, YOU must decide where to eat on a date (don't let her choose the restaurant!), you mustn't be afraid to eat first (although social conventions do dictate that we must wait for both our plates to be served!), and you should get the best bites. If you're splitting a piece of cheesecake, for example, don't be afraid to dig in and get the best portion! The girl will actually respect you for it, much more so than if you bashfully gave up the best piece to her. Again, retain your position as the "top dog."

This is a dangerous and demeaning concept. Scientists no longer routinely use the term *alpha* even when speaking of wolves. They say "breeding male" and "breeding female" or "father and mother." They realize that the term *alpha,* as misappropriated, implies that the individual fought to obtain dominance, an assumption that simply isn't true. David Mech, arguably the world's leading expert on wolf behavior, said in his article "Whatever Happened to the Term Alpha Wolf,"

Rather than viewing a wolf pack as a group of animals orga-nized with a "top dog" that fought its way to the top, or a male-female pair of such aggressive wolves, science has come to understand that most wolf packs are merely family groups formed exactly the same way as human families are formed.

Although wolf researchers have known better for many years, a vast number of dog people, even professional trainers, are still quite enamored with the concept. When I was searching online for a trainer to help my sister with her dog in South Florida, the first site I visited had a colossal banner reading, IS YOUR DOG WEARING THE PANTS IN THE FAMILY? Obviously, the phrase *wearing the pants* was meant to indicate that the dog had somehow taken control, but consider for a moment what it means to be in charge. First and foremost, the one in charge is responsible for his own well-being and the well-being of all those in his care. Because our dogs cannot provide their own healthcare, shelter, toys, and food, it would appear that humans have the upper hand. Our dogs already know that; people seem to be the ones struggling with the concept.

It is true that dogs can be bossy and demanding, but poor behavior should in no way suggest that dogs are plotting the subjugation of the human race. The belief that dogs seek to take charge of their owners leads me to shake my head in wonder. Our dogs know that we are their parent figures. We should spend more time worrying about being a good parent and less about who goes through the door first.

Who goes through the door first: For those trainers who believe we must dominate our dogs, the doorway issue seems to be significant. They contend that a dog who goes out the door first is trying to dominate his human. I've had many good trainers tell me that they've seen improvement in a dog's behavior when owners began demanding the dog let them go through a doorway first. Although I believe them, I know it has nothing to do with dominance and everything to do with instilling more impulse control in the dog.

Higher and higher: Jumping on people is also considered a dominance behavior by many trainers. Some believe that dogs are "height seeking" as a way to gain power. This is simply not the case. Dogs jump on people to get close to human faces. In wolf packs, supplicants lick the faces of their elders either in deference or in the hope that those licks might encourage the elder to regurgitate food. Dogs who jump up are not trying to dominate you, they're greeting you.

Eat first and be the boss: "Leaders must eat first" is yet another often-mentioned theory from some trainers. The contention is that alpha wolves always eat first, again a false conclusion from faulty information. They do not. Depending on the season, the youngest puppies might well be the first to eat. In reality, your meal would likely be more peaceful if you fed the dog first. Then, even if he still begs at the table, you can take comfort in knowing that he isn't as close to starvation as his pathetic appearance might lead you to believe.

Who's walking whom: Many trainers also claim that if a dog walks in front of his owner, he's displaying dominance. They believe that the leader of a wolf pack always goes first. Once again, this is incorrect. When hunting, the pack follows the member who has the best line on the prey. The idea that walking ahead is dominance is nonsense. Dogs on walks are usually excited and pull ahead in their enthusiasm.

Recently, Cesar Millan publicly criticized President Obama for allowing Bo, the First Dog, to walk in front of him. He proclaimed, "Day one was not a good scene—the dog always in front of the President of the United States." His comments were reported by media outlets worldwide as if they were somehow highly credible instead of absolute lunacy, which they were. Perhaps it would be a good idea if President Obama could help Bo learn not to pull on his leash, a task easily accomplished, but only because it would help Bo focus on the person at the other end of the leash, making the walk more of a team activity. But regardless of Bo's position when walking with the president, I do not expect to wake up tomorrow morning to find that Bo has gained the upper hand and is leash-walking President Obama. Dogs simply do not operate that way. Dominance doesn't work that way, either.

Dominance is a term that scientists use to describe which of two or more members of the same species has priority access to valuable resources, such as food and water. It isn't possible for a dog to gain priority access in the human world, because they have virtually no control over their environment. Dominance is a complicated issue— what is valuable to one animal on one day may not be of similar value the next. Labeling dominance in the appropriate context is a difficult, convoluted process for researchers, having no bearing whatsoever on the relationship between humans and dogs. We are members of different species, and what is valuable to each of us is quite different.

Worst of all, *dominance* implies an adversarial relationship, placing people on one team and dogs on another. This is a terrible loss for the people, who miss the opportunity to experience the joy of teaming up with their dogs. It is unfortunate for the dogs as well, often with more serious consequences.

Not long ago, I received an email about a Great Pyrenees from my friend Lauren. The four-year-old dog, Baron, lived with a family consisting of a mother, father, and two young sons. The dog had gotten along well with the mother and kids, but not with the father. Baron had actually bitten the father a few days earlier, and now the family felt they had to surrender the dog to rescue. Lauren thought I might be able to help mitigate the situation, perhaps even convince the father to give Baron another chance.

I went to visit the family at their home in Atlanta's upscale Buckhead neighborhood. Given Baron's reported dislike for the man, I was prepared to find the dad a gruff, unpleasant sort. He was nothing of the kind. He was charming, intelligent, and clearly saddened by the situation with the dog. It took only a few moments to uncover what had happened. The father, in an effort to be a good dog owner, bought books and watched television shows to learn how best to handle a big dog such as Baron. The advice he found dictated that he demonstrate to Baron who was the boss by executing moves such as the alpha roll (where the dog is pinned on his back to the floor) and stare-downs. The relationship had deteriorated over the few weeks that Baron had lived with the family. Ultimately, the father's guidance was so flawed that his own dog feared him enough to bite.

The damage done was in no way confined to the small puncture wound on the father's forearm, the only physical mark from the experience. The father ended up so afraid of his dog that he could no longer allow Baron to remain in the house. Thanks to the teachings of Cesar Millan and others like him, Baron lost his home, and two little boys lost the dog they loved.

For years I've understood the danger of the dominance model

from a theoretical perspective. As I drove away from the house and the sobbing children, with the handsome Great Pyrenees whining pathetically from the backseat, the theoretical became intensely personal.

My husband believes that the alpha philosophy, such as it is, can be summed up concisely: *Everything a dog ever does is because of dominance, and the only solution is dominance.* This defines the model with terrible accuracy, and it is a dangerous concept for dogs and people. Ask any rescue group, and I'll wager that the number of dogs turned in for biting has risen dramatically over the past five years. I know that it has in golden retriever rescue organizations. It is not a coincidence that the number of dog-bite incidents has increased since the alpha concept became popular. Our dogs are now afraid of us. And, in turn, we have become afraid of them.

CHAPTER NINE

Pick of the Litter

Fortunately for us, dogs are perhaps the most forgiving species on the planet. Forming a lasting, extraordinary relationship with a dog is a simple process if you do one thing—*bond*. The connection is everything, a dictum we live by at Canine Assistants.

The traditional moniker of the relationship, *dog and owner,* has been the topic of much discussion over the past few years. In fact, there has been a movement, underwritten by certain factions within the dog world, to rename the relationship, declaring *dog and guardian* more appropriate. The notion of being a dog's guardian rather than his owner seems innocuous enough at first glance. But when I looked into what was behind this change in terminology, I learned there was more to it than simple semantics.

Some claim this change in terminology is merely a way to promote increased respect for companion animals. Certainly there is a benefit in our words reflecting greater respect for animals. However, others charge that the effort is promoted by radical animal-rights organizations who will not stop there but will attempt to pass laws

incrementally bestowing humanlike rights on animals that will ultimately liberate them from our guardianship.

I, for one, know my dogs will want no part of such an effort.
They have no interest in sleeping on the cold ground and scavenging meager food from dumps instead of sleeping on my warm bed
and eating the good food I provide them—of this I am certain.

Dogs are a species dependent on humans and, consequently, we
cannot help but interfere in their lives. A good life is not possible for
dogs without our care, and those who seek to "save by liberation"
are endangering the safety of the very animals whom they profess to
defend.

That said, I am in favor of anything that encourages people to be
kinder to their animals. I also support making the abuse of an animal
a felony, with stiff penalties and consistent enforcement. I do not
consider my animals items that I own. They are my friends, part of
my family, and my responsibility. I would not want to live in a world
without golden retrievers or Great Pyrenees or Chihuahuas. Puppy
mills should be forced out of business through the enactment of
more and tougher regulations, but I do not want responsible breeders forced out along with them. Adopting a dog from a rescue organization or shelter is a wonderful, noble way to give a dog another
chance at a good life. But I also understand, and in no way con-
demn, those who want to obtain a dog through a responsible breeder.

Breeders must focus on breeding healthier dogs (as many good
breeders already do) and not allow the human desire for superficial
physical traits to cause suffering, such as in bulldogs and other
brachycephalic (flat-faced) breeds that struggle to breathe. Over
time, deformities have become the standard for particular breeds,
causing a great deal of suffering simply for the sake of appearance.
We should return to the days when function was more important
than form in breeds.

CHOOSING RIGHT

One of the most important steps to developing a strong connection
with a dog is choosing the right dog in the first place. You can be

an "owner," "a guardian," or "a parent" to your dog, as long as that means that you will do all in your power to give him a wonderful life. The good news is that if you already have a dog, it's probably the correct one, because something attracted you to him initially. But if you're thinking about bringing a new dog into your home, there are some important factors to consider when deciding which one to choose.

Select the type of dog you think would do best in your world; specifically, what energy level you can and want to handle. If you are a couch potato, border collie–like enthusiasm will probably drive you crazy. Conversely, if you're an outdoor enthusiast who exercises daily, a laid-back dog, such as a mastiff, will most likely not suit. Although it is important to take the size of your living space into consideration, do not assume that a small breed will automatically fit a small apartment and that a large breed requires a big house with a yard. Breed propensity and individual characteristics are much more important than size, so do your research.

Individual dogs don't always follow their breed description but, more likely than not, they will. If you have children, you need to find a dog who loves kids, so, logically, you will have a better chance of finding the right dog if you look at breeds and mixes known for their friendliness. If you enjoy entertaining and have lots of company, you'll want a dog who isn't wary of strangers. The AKC website has excellent information on the various breeds and what you can expect from them.

PUPPIES

After deciding on a breed, the next decision is whether to get a puppy or an adult dog. There are definite advantages to a puppy. Puppies are cute, so you tend to bond with them more quickly and easily. The youth and cuteness factor also means that you might be more tolerant of their mistakes than you would be of an adult dog's. Although they do come with genetic and temperamental propensities, puppies are as close as you can get to a blank canvas. This gives you the opportunity to control, at least partially, what they will be like as a finished work. For example, taking the time to socialize your puppy will ensure that he has good bite inhibition.

If you are looking for a purebred puppy, a reputable breeder is your best option. Those who have purchased dogs from a breeder in the past are the best source of reference. Check with anyone you know who has the breed that you're interested in or find a community online to see if they can offer counsel. You can also query your local veterinary clinic and groomers for suggestions on reputable breeders. Find a breeder near your home if at all possible.

Many good breeders have waiting lists, so you might be required to place a deposit on the puppy even in advance of its birth. Before making that commitment, arrange to visit the breeder's home or kennel. Be sure the place is clean and the dogs appear healthy and well cared for. Expect to be asked a number of questions about yourself and your environment; a good breeder will interview you extensively. Below is a list of questions you should ask in return.

- **May I see the paperwork for the genetic testing you have had done on the puppy's parents?** Study the common problems of your desired breed before your visit so you know which tests should have been done. If the breeder says he doesn't test because he has never had problems with his dogs' bloodline, leave. All good breeders check to be certain they are not passing on negative health issues to future generations.
- **Do you do any early stimulation with your puppies, such as Super Dog?** Studies have shown that pups handled this way demonstrate an increased capacity for learning, improved cardiovascular performance, stronger heartbeats, stronger adrenal glands, more tolerance to stress, and greater resistance to disease. The Super Dog protocol consists of five exercises, done for five seconds each, that stimulate puppies' neurological development when done from day 3 to day 17 of life. See Appendix E.
- **When do you let your dogs go home?** The answer should be at eight weeks or later.

- **What socialization is done prior to the puppies' leaving?** Some breeders, concerned about illness, will isolate puppies. If your breeder does this, you will have to supersocialize your pup from the moment you get your hands on him.
- **May I have several references?** If the breeder refuses, you should be concerned. If he does provide a list, contact the references before concluding your purchase, inquiring about health, personality, and any other issues they may have experienced. Try to contact as many references as possible.
- **What is your return policy?** Not that you are going to want to return your precious pup, but a good breeder will always take back a puppy, no matter how long you have had him.

An alternative to a breeder is a local breed-specific rescue program. Although you might not know much detail on the puppies' backgrounds, you will be helping puppies in need and, if they are young enough, you will still be able to cultivate good socialization and bite inhibition.

When evaluating a litter of puppies, it is almost impossible not to fall in love with every one of them, so it might be difficult to select which puppy should become a member of your family. Decide whether you want a male or a female or if you are willing to go with either sex. Also, *before* you meet the puppies, resolve what personality type will best suit you and everyone else living in your household. If you have children, you'll want a dog who is neither excessively bold nor shy. You are looking for that rock-solid type who falls in the middle. If you are a go-getter who loves to try new things, you will be happiest with a puppy who is outgoing and self-confident. If you feel more comfortable in familiar surroundings and hesitate to try new things, you might do best with a puppy who shares your traits. You will still need to socialize him well, but you are more likely to be in tune when he starts to get stimulation overload. Your similarities will help you empathize with your puppy, especially in this situation, where a more assertive person might blithely forge ahead, not realizing the puppy was having an internal meltdown.

When trying to assess a puppy's personality, ask the breeder or adoption group *not* to provide you with their insights until you have done your own assessment. That way, you will be more likely to form an unbiased opinion. (Note: Puppies who are the only ones in their litters, known as singletons, can have significant behavior issues and should be adopted only by an experienced dog owner.) Assess puppies when they are at least four weeks of age, moving around easily and eating some solid food. Ask the breeder or adoption group at what time the puppies are usually awake, and make your appointment accordingly. A group of sleeping puppies nestled into a pile is cute, but having to wake them for your assessment might throw off the results, as some normally active pups might still be sleepy. Bring a small fleece squeaky toy with you. Be sure the toy is new, because you don't want to spread germs to unvaccinated puppies. You should also bring a large trash bag stuffed with shredded newspaper or leaves, and a tin can with four coins in it.

When you arrive, stand quietly out of sight for several minutes, watching the puppies interact with their siblings. The puppies who move around most actively, investigating the pen and wrestling with siblings, are the ones most likely to be outgoing. The puppies who watch the action from a distance are most likely to be more introverted.

Enter the room quietly, and see how each puppy reacts to your presence. At this point, do not say anything, make eye contact, or even smile—just stand there as benignly as possible. The puppies who try to engage you without prompting are likely highly social in nature.

After remaining silent for thirty seconds or so, squat down with a big smile on your face, and in a happy tone say, "Pup, pup, puppies," noticing how each reacts. A puppy who does not make some movement toward you or attempt to make eye contact is probably not very social.

These first few assessments should allow you to narrow the

search to several favorites for further evaluation. Each of the remaining tests should be conducted on one puppy at a time, away from his littermates, and can be done either inside or outside.

When first removing a puppy from his littermates, be sure to give him a moment to relieve himself outside. After that, hold him in your arms and lightly run your fingers over his body. Tug gently at his toes, tail, and ears. If he struggles vigorously in your arms or reacts strongly to your tugging, he most likely does not have a laid-back personality.

Gently roll the puppy over on his back in your arms, cradling him close to your body so that he doesn't feel as if he's going to fall. If he struggles, speak in soothing tones while gently rocking him back and forth as you would an infant. Notice if he settles or becomes even more frantic to get down. Puppies who settle well with human touch tend to be easier to handle than those who do not.

Now put the puppy down and toss your fleece toy for him. Does he chase it? If not, wiggle it to make certain he sees it and that it has his attention. If he still shows no interest in the toy, he might be an especially shy personality type who will require extra TLC to help navigate the world.

Next drag out the trash bag filled with newspaper for him to inspect. Observe whether he walks up and pounces on it or runs from it. If he initially shies away, does he eventually come back to inspect it with your encouragement? It's okay (and understandable) if a puppy feels nervous when seeing something new, but you want him to recover quickly. If he remains afraid of the trash bag and didn't investigate the toy, take the puppy back to his littermates. When you put him down, does he move away from you quickly or sit looking up at you? If he moves away, this is a puppy who will need considerable help learning to trust humans.

If your puppy does fairly well with the trash bag, wait until his attention is focused elsewhere, and then drop your tin can containing the four coins from a height of no more than one foot. You want the can to make noise when it falls, but not a loud one. (Using scary noises to startle dogs, as is sometimes suggested for interrupting unwanted behavior, is not a good idea. Dogs can become overly sensitive to noises very easily, creating phobias that are difficult to treat.) Note how the puppy reacts to the sound. If he does not look toward the can at all, repeat the drop from a slightly higher position. Once again, check to see if he moves toward the can or runs from it. Being momentarily startled is okay, as long as the puppy recovers quickly.

Ask the owner or foster if you can feed him a few pieces of his puppy kibble. Drop most of the pieces into his bowl, but hold a few in reserve. As soon as you put the bowl down directly in front of the puppy, pick it back up. Repeat the exercise, but this time move more slowly as you reach to pick up the bowl. Be cautious, watching to see any indication that the puppy is going to snap at you. If so, stop immediately. Dogs who guard their food at an early age can be helped, but the process takes great patience. Consider carefully before adopting a puppy who seems angry when you pick up his bowl. If the puppy is happy to let you have it, drop another few pieces of kibble in it and replace it in front of him.

Finally, take the puppy back to his littermates. He has been away and will need a short time to greet his siblings. After a moment, squat down and call out, "Pup, pup, puppy." If your puppy comes over to see you immediately, he enjoyed your interaction and is looking for more.

Remember to be true to your own personality. If you are shy, perhaps the shy puppy captures your heart. These suggested assessments are meant only to uncover characteristics of the puppies, not dissuade you from choosing the one you feel is best for you.

Once you pick your puppy, start assembling those things you will need when he is ready to come home:

- **puppy food.** If you want to change his food, bring home a small bag of the kibble your puppy started on and wean him over by mixing in the new—approximately one-eighth of the total amount fed at a time, eight times until the switch is completed. Slow down the process if his stomach seems sensitive to the transition.
- **one bowl for food and one or two for water.**

- **a crate, an exercise pen, or both.**
- **your veterinary clinic's phone number and the number of the nearest emergency clinic.**
- **toys,** including hollow toys for stuffing with food, puzzle toys for entertainment, squeaky toys for interactive play, tug toys, and dog-safe balls.
- **a leash and a harness or collar for walks.**
- **a plastic safety collar for identification.**

It is also a good idea to write down the rules of the house, as a reminder to yourself and anyone else living with you. Is it okay for your puppy to climb on the furniture, or would you prefer he not? Where will the puppy sleep? Will you use a crate for your puppy? If not, how do you plan to contain him? Puppies are like crawling babies: You must either focus solely on them or safely corral them somewhere. My favorite setup is a small exercise pen with an open crate inside. This is used to keep them safe and should never be used for punishment.

Put newspapers down in the pen if you must leave the puppy for a longer time than he could realistically be expected not to have an accident. I use the age of a puppy in months as a guideline for how long he should be able to refrain from relieving himself. So, a two-month-old puppy can be expected to last two hours in between trips outside. I use their age in months plus three hours for overnight expectations, provided they have emptied their bladder and bowels just before bed. Consistency is essential with puppies, so stick to your schedule, and be sure all family members comply with household rules, avoiding confusion for the puppy.

Housebreaking is all about showing the puppy where you want him to relieve himself and then being certain he is taken to that spot when he needs to go. Puppies have to go to the bathroom immediately after waking up from a nap or overnight sleep, after eating, and any other time they have spent more hours than their age in months (as noted, two hours for a two-month-old puppy) without going. You do not have time to do *anything* else before you take your puppy outside, especially if he has just awakened.

Always go outside with your puppy until he is well toilet-trained. Take yummy treats along so that you can praise and reward him afterward. Encourage your puppy to walk in small circles with you while giving him whatever cue word you've chosen to indicate he should relieve himself. We use *Better hurry* at Canine Assistants. If your puppy doesn't go when you take him out, try again in thirty minutes. Once he does go, do not take him back to his bathroom spot until it is time for his next potty break. This helps him understand what to do and where. Otherwise, he simply thinks you are taking him for a walk. If your dog has an accident in the house, clean it up with a product especially designed to eliminate pet stain odors. *Do not* punish the dog for accidents. If you did not see him, it is too late for him to understand your irritation, and therefore cruel. If you do catch him in the act, you can say, "ainck!" (the wounded-duck noise) to startle him, then dash him outside. However, do not frighten him; the last thing you want is a dog who is afraid of relieving himself in front of you.

Puppies also need to learn from the beginning that an open door or gate is not an invitation to bolt through it. Begin teaching your puppy to "wait" the first day you bring him home. As you turn your doorknob and open your door, put your hand on your puppy's chest and tell him to "wait" for a count of two; then say, "Go through." The *Wait . . . Go through* exercise should be repeated every time you go through a door or gate. Gradually ease your hand away from your pup's chest as he begins to understand the word *wait*. Eventually, waiting should be automatic until you say, "Go through."

CHEWING

Understand that all dogs, but puppies in particular, need to chew. If you leave your shoes out where an unattended puppy can get them, they are fair game. Puppies are not born knowing what is acceptable to chew in the human world. When you catch your puppy gnawing on something inappropriate, calmly exchange that item with one of his chew toys. I like to label each toy for my dogs with a name such as Bear, and when trading a bad chew toy for a good one, I say,

"Let's go get Bear." I do this so that as a puppy gets older, I can say "ainck!" when he starts chewing on something inappropriate and tell him to go get his Bear.

Bite inhibition is the single most important thing you can teach your puppy. If your puppy play-bites, take steps to cultivate bite inhibition. Example: When he nips you hard enough to hurt, yelp loudly to startle the puppy and turn away from him for a long count of five. You are telling the pup that your skin is sensitive and that you will not play with him if he is going to hurt you. Then turn back and begin playing until he nips you again. Repeat as necessary.

As your puppy begins to ease up on the amount of pressure he uses when he mouths you, begin acting as if any pressure is painful. Yelp and turn away as you did with nips that actually hurt. Now you are telling him that any bite is painful so he must be very careful with you. Teaching your puppy not to bite down on humans may one day save his life, because he will most likely never break the skin on a person—even if reflexively biting when in pain.

SOCIALIZATION

For years, people were told not to let their puppies out into the world until their vaccination cycles had been completed. We now know better. Puppies become easily comfortable with new experiences until approximately twelve weeks of age, when the window of socialization typically closes. You should introduce your puppy to every new sight, smell, noise, person, and animal you possibly can by the twelve-week mark. In Appendix F, I have suggested a list of things to which you should attempt to expose your puppy before the opportunity passes.

In deference to his vulnerable immune system, do not take your puppy to places such as pet stores or dog parks. Expose him only to other dogs you are confident have been fully vaccinated. Be sure the other dogs he meets are gentle and kind so he won't be frightened, although a correction for inappropriate behavior from an adult dog is okay. Also, puppies go through a sensitive period at around eight weeks of age. His exposure to new things should therefore be positive experiences, because bad ones at that age might leave an indelible impression. Most dogs also go through another period of high anxiety, usually between six and eight months of age. Early exposures are critical, but the continued introduction of new sights, sounds, and experiences are vital for a truly well-socialized dog.

Also, take your puppy to the veterinarian *before* he has to get his shots, so that he can have a fun first visit. Bring along a bath mat from home for every vet appointment so that he doesn't slip on the examining table. Remember to hold a puppy in your arms who has yet to finish his vaccinations, except when you put him on the bath mat in the examining room. Keep visits, especially his first, upbeat, giving him much praise and many small treats, so that he knows good things happen while at the vet.

If your puppy will require a professional groomer, it is a good idea to make a few pleasant, uneventful trips to that facility as well. Once again, take along your bath mat for that comforting smell of home.

If your puppy is of a breed that normally has its ears or tails cropped, you should contemplate a few things before you schedule the surgery. Ethicists recommend you base what is fair for your dog on your answers to the following questions.

1. If the dog could understand, would he choose the procedure for himself?

2. Would a comparable procedure be acceptable in children?

3. Is it necessary for his well-being?

4. If the procedure were not currently being done, would society find it acceptable if it were introduced now?

5. Would arguments in support of the procedure be equally valid if applied to a comparable procedure on another part of the body? For example, if it is acceptable to crop his ears, is it equally acceptable to crop his lips?

Tail docking and ear cropping are now banned in many countries. I find both barbaric. Ear cropping especially seems extremely painful for dogs, and my husband would be unwilling to do such procedures if he were still in private practice. Clinics will often keep the dog overnight so they can have stronger pain medications for the first twenty-four hours. Although some dogs appear more stoic about pain, why cause them any at all if not necessary? Puppies deserve our protection, especially from the whims of fashion.

Spaying and neutering are also elective surgeries. The difference is that spays and neuters prevent or reduce some very real threats to our dogs.

Neuters (male)

> prevent prostatic hyperplasia, infection, cancer
> prevent testicular cancer, orchitis, trauma
> prevent venereal diseases—brucellosis, transmissible venereal tumors
> prevent unwanted litters
> decrease roaming by 90 percent
> decrease aggressive behavior with other males by approximatcly 60 percent
> decrease mounting behaviors by approximately 70 percent
> lessen chance of involvement in human bites

Spays (female)

> if performed before first heat, almost guarantee females will not get mammary cancer
> prevent pyometra, a uterine infection that can be fatal
> prevent heats every six months and discharge all over the house
> prevent unwanted litters
> prevent venereal diseases—brucellosis, transmissible venereal tumors

Life is so much safer for a dog who is spayed or neutered that it is irresponsible not to have it done. Spays and neuters are routinely performed on puppies as young as eight weeks of age with no apparent ill effects, but discuss when to do this with your veterinarian. Consider how early you're comfortable with having your puppy anesthetized. I prefer to wait until my pups are five or six months old before subjecting them to surgery, but that is a personal preference.

Puppies are wonderful creatures, but life with a pup is not easy. They require a tremendous time commitment, constant supervision, and patient instruction. If you don't have the time to devote to raising a puppy correctly, you might be better off with an adult dog.

CHAPTER TEN

Adopting an Adult Dog

I love puppies: They're cute, playful, and full of potential. But there's something special about adult dogs that I adore. They have a grace and majesty that comes with age and experience. When you look into their eyes, you can see much of what they have seen. Take on a puppy and you get a baby to nurture and guide; adopt an adult dog and you get a friend.

Adult dogs have several major advantages over puppies. They are largely finished works, so you know, for the most part, what you are getting in terms of personality. Adult dogs don't have to be taken outside for bathroom breaks as often, and they don't require the same level of supervision. And when you choose an adult dog, you are probably giving a home to one who needs it.

The primary disadvantage of adopting an adult dog is that he will come with baggage. Having to find a new home, regardless of the reason, is traumatic. Add the fact that many adult dogs available for adoption have come from less than optimal situations, and you can readily see that adult dogs can come with issues. Being aware of these issues in advance will help considerably, so where to go to find your dog is important.

Rescue groups are a great resource when looking for an adult dog. Information on available dogs is often posted on websites such as petfinder.com. Most rescue programs use foster homes, and foster parents can provide a wealth of information. In addition, good organizations will have done an extensive veterinary check, so you are more likely to know what kinds of health problems a dog has. Do not be surprised if the rescue group puts you through an adoption evaluation that rivals one for a human child, including a home visit and reference request. The dogs in their care have lost at least one home, and they make great efforts to ensure that doesn't happen again.

Most local shelters also post information about available dogs on the Internet. Shelters can vary widely in the type of assessment they conduct on the dogs in their care. Some do a fantastic job, while others simply don't have the time or money, so it is buyer beware to some extent. That said, some of the best dogs I've known, the dog who was my greatest teacher, my forever dog, Nicholas, came from a county shelter. So don't be put off, just be careful.

When evaluating an adult dog for adoption at Canine Assistants, we use the following test.

1. Watch the dog from a distance to see if he appears aloof or friendly to passersby.

2. Approach the dog sideways. Do not speak or smile, just be neutral. See if he approaches you.

3. Now turn and face the dog, kneel, and give him a big smile and a happy greeting to see what reaction this elicits.

4. Watch someone else walk the dog on-leash to see how much attention he pays to his human handler.

5. Find a quiet spot where you can sit in a chair with the dog off-leash (or on a long leash if the area is not safely enclosed). Does the dog come back to visit you fairly quickly?

6. As long as you feel totally safe, lightly run your hands all over his body. If he is okay with that, check his ears and inside his mouth. Will he let you handle his paws?

7. When he is distracted, knock loudly on a wall. Does he bark? If so, how long before he quiets down?

8. Try handing him a small treat. Does he grab it from you or take it gently? If he grabs the first treat forcefully, tell him to "be gentle" by holding more of the next treat in your hand, refusing to give it to him until he's using his mouth nicely. A dog who grabs treats and has trouble quickly grasping the notion of *gentle* may be difficult to manage later. I cannot claim that there is a scientific correlation between resource guarding and grabbing treats, but my experience says there is.

9. Introduce the dog to everyone in your family. If you have children, you want him to look at them as if saying, "Where have you been? I've been waiting for you!" The only dogs who are truly good with children are those who have grown up with children.

10. If you have another dog or cat, see how the dog interacts with similar animals.

Temperament tests given only once tell you almost nothing, other than how that dog reacted at a particular time, in a particular location, on a particular day. Many shelters are now using a temperament test that includes taking food away from a dog while he is eating, to measure his resource-guarding tendencies. As mentioned earlier, I realize that tough decisions must be made in shelters because of limited space, but the testing should offer a fair assessment of the dog. For that reason, I do not like the artificial-hand test—a rubber hand attached to a wooden rod used to examine dogs for aggressiveness while they're eating.

The idea is to protect evaluators from dogs who might react in a hostile manner when someone tries to take away their food. Of course, I understand the need to safeguard workers, but the artificial hand is such an oddity to the dogs that it does not give them a reasonable chance. The hand does not look or smell like a human hand, so dogs have no way to understand what is happening during the test. The testers I have watched pester the dog by "patting" him first with the hand before lowering it toward the food. They yank it away several times, finally placing the hand directly into the bowl.

One of the dogs I witnessed being tested merely grabbed the hand as if to say, "Stop it." In my opinion, she was not the least bit aggressive. Unfortunately, the dog's owner did not solicit my opinion until after she had had her dog euthanized, based on the recommendation of the trainer who administered the test. In the majority of shelter situations, dogs who react to the artificial hand, even by mouthing it gently, are labeled aggressive and destroyed. Conversely, it is possible that some dogs who might have actually bitten a human hand did not bite the artificial one because they simply didn't know what it was. There must be a better way to identify resource guarders, although admittedly I have not thought (or heard) of one yet.

Because testing cannot always tell us everything, it is critical to treat any adult dog you bring into your home as if he has resource- and collar-guarding issues. Go through the desensitization exercises in chapter 7 when you first arrive home with a new dog. If your dog clearly has no problem with the drills, you can progress quickly, but do not skip them. Everyone in your home, especially children, should do the exercises to reinforce correct behavior, once you feel confident that the dog is safe.

When you adopt an adult dog, you usually get what is known as a "honeymoon" period that lasts anywhere from a few days to a month. This is the time when your dog is adjusting to new surroundings and circumstances and his normal behavior may be somewhat inhibited. Use the honeymoon period to help him understand what is expected.

Everything that applies to bringing home a new puppy applies to a new adult dog as well, so review the advice in the previous chapter about bringing puppies into your house. The singular difference is that you can expect adult dogs to last longer between bathroom breaks and require less supervision after being acclimated to the house rules.

If you already have a dog, introduce him to your new dog by taking both for a walk on-leash, side by side. Then, in a neutral place, such as a neighbor's fenced yard, turn both dogs loose. If one is far larger than the other, you must have an experienced trainer on hand unless you're absolutely certain the larger dog is friendly with smaller dogs. Caution suggests having a sizeable towel available to throw over the larger dog's head if he goes after the little one.

It is best not to restrain either dog, but you can leave a leash trailing loosely on both if you'd prefer. When the dogs first meet, stay quiet and allow them to smell each other as is customary. If two dogs of the same size start to scuffle, *remain quiet,* because any shouting will only add emotional energy to an already overcharged situation. Try to brave it out for several minutes and see if the dogs come to their own resolution. Dogfights sound horrible, but rarely is any real damage done. I feel safe allowing two dogs of approximately the same size to fight it out as long as their teeth stay near each other's necks. The most dangerous attacks on dogs of similar size generally target the stomach and back legs. Some males will engage in a mock battle to determine how well the other dog recognizes signals and abides by the rules.

If the fight goes on for more than two minutes, or it begins to be too much for you, throw your towel over one dog's head. Note: **Do not** put any part of your body close to either dog's mouth to avoid being bitten in the fray; dog skin is much tougher than ours. If the towel trick does not work and you have another person with you, try grabbing both dogs by the back legs to pull them apart. This is a move of last resort, in my opinion. If one dog is holding on to the other, pulling them apart will cause a ripping injury to the one being held. If you stay quiet and calm, it is most likely that any scuffle will be over before you feel the need to intervene.

This is not a fight to determine an alpha but rather to establish ground rules for future interaction. There is status among dogs. Such status is the canine equivalent of which child gets to sit in the good chair or pick the movie. Some dogs want to be the big brother or big sister and other dogs don't care. Many multiple-dog families will notice that the roles switch according to the activity. My dog Jack is all about sleeping on the bed, and he will growl if Butch attempts to join him. Butch, on the other hand, is the king of the toys and thinks nothing of hoarding them all. Dogs need to learn what is important to one another in order to live together peacefully.

SOMEONE FOR EVERYONE

Not long after I started Canine Assistants, my friend Traci and I pulled in to the parking lot of our local minimart. As we got out of the car, we simultaneously spotted an animal considerably larger than a cat gracelessly darting behind the store's dumpster. My first reaction was that it was a large fox; Traci thought it was a small coyote. Of course we had to investigate. Cautiously we approached what turned out to be a mostly toothless, quite elderly, three-legged beagle-type dog.

The dog's filthy coat and emaciated appearance led us to believe that he was a stray. No one in the store seemed to know where the dog had come from, but apparently he had been hanging around the dumpster for days. As kindness and karma demanded, we took him back to Canine Assistants. He became known as Toothless Joe—Joe for short.

At a time when the monthly cost of dog food was already overwhelming, Toothless Joe's presence at Canine Assistants was something of a problem. In addition, a veterinary exam indicated that the dog was in the early stages of heart failure. What were we to do with him? Clearly, we couldn't train an old, toothless, three-legged dog with a heart condition to assist anyone, but we couldn't find anyone willing to take Toothless Joe in as a pet, either.

Several weeks later, something miraculous happened. Mary, our recipient services coordinator, answered the phone. I overheard her say, "Well, Sergeant Aimes, we just might have a dog for you." Taking a long breath, she continued. "But he does have a few issues." As she listed each of Joe's problems, she paused to listen to the man's response. Mary's voice grew more and more incredulous. When the call finally concluded, she burst out laughing.

"You will not believe this!" was the first thing out of her mouth. The elderly man on the phone had just been released from the VA hospital after being there for many months. One of the staff doctors suggested that he get a dog to keep him company, because his wife had recently passed away and he had no family. Although the idea of a dog was appealing, he was seventy-eight and in poor health and had neither the energy nor the inclination to take on a young dog. He was calling to see if we knew of an older dog looking for a home. Indeed, we did, Mary told him. But there were issues. First, she informed him that Toothless Joe had a heart condition. No problem, he countered. He too had a heart condition. It was the very reason he had been in the VA hospital. But also, Joe didn't have any teeth. That didn't bother him; he had just gotten dentures himself. Finally, Mary noted that Joe had only three legs. The man shouted for joy and exclaimed, "Between the two of us we'll have a full four, then. I lost a leg in the war!"

Sergeant Aimes and Toothless Joe met that very afternoon, and the connection was immediate and powerful. As of that first day together, neither of them was expected to live more than a year. But somehow they seemed to keep each other going. It was more than five years later that Sergeant Aimes and Toothless Joe died . . . within a week of each other.

Consider opening your heart to an older dog who needs a home. Approximately 25 percent of the people who turn their dogs in to shelters do so because the dogs are too old. Other than past the point of death, what constitutes "too old"? I adore older dogs. And while some assert that older dogs have higher healthcare costs, I'm not sure that's true. Routine vet care for a puppy is more expensive than for an older dog, and young dogs are much more likely to get hurt. You might have to pay for some arthritis medicine, but that is well worth it when you consider that most older dogs don't need much training and get into much less trouble. During the past twenty years at Canine Assistants, I have learned that there is a perfect dog for everyone. Just ask Toothless Joe.

CHAPTER ELEVEN

The Ties That Bind

A strong connection will give you patience as you guide your dog through life on Planet Human, where he doesn't speak the language or understand the customs. It's what will give your dog the desire to please a member of an entirely different species. I have been fortunate enough to be a part of generating more than a thousand new human-dog relationships at Canine Assistants, and that experience has taught me some important rules for creating and maintaining a strong bond.

Establish a routine. Routine is comforting for people and dogs. When your dog understands that breakfast is served at seven A.M. Monday through Friday and at nine A.M. on Saturday and Sunday, he is less likely to irritate you by asking for breakfast earlier. Keeping your dog on a set schedule for things such as feeding, walking, resting, and playing means that your dog will have fewer housebreaking accidents and drive you less batty asking to play.

Dogs settle into a routine fairly quickly, and in some ways, it becomes like a promise you have made them. The more you are able to "keep your promises" by staying on schedule, the more your dog will trust you and be better able to handle occasional variations to the schedule with grace.

Show respect, and expect respect in return. Show your dog respect by treating him well, and invariably he will do the same for you. Be courteous to your dog. Expect him to return that courtesy by waiting before going through doors and gates, coming when called, and exhibiting nice manners. Understand that respect is in no way related to fear.

Not long ago, someone emailed me a picture of two dogs. One had his mouth open and relaxed, his ears up, and a look of cheerful anticipation. Under his photo was a caption: "This is a dominant dog. If your dog looks like this, show him who is boss before it's too late." The other photo depicted a dog with his head down, his mouth tightly closed, and his ears slicked back. Although it is difficult to tell in a photograph, the dog seemed to be moving in a crouched position toward the person holding the camera. The caption under this one said, "This is a submissive dog."

The captions on both photographs were dangerous *nonsense*. The first dog was a willing, happy fellow. I hardly think that his expression of confidence was an indication that he was planning to overthrow the local government. As I have said before, *dominance* and *submission* are ridiculously inappropriate concepts when it comes to describing the human-dog relationship, unless you plan on fighting with your dog over resources you already control.

The dog in the second photograph was afraid. He was clearly offering appeasing, please-don't-be-mad-at-me behaviors. It is pathetic that some people see this as a positive demeanor, that there are adult human beings who enjoy making dogs feel afraid. These people are abusers, and their actions should be accorded no acceptance from society.

Establish small rituals. Develop simple habits between you and your dog. In my house, all the dogs do a sit before bed, I say goodnight, and then I give them each a small piece of cheese. It is just a silly little pattern we fell into when one of my dogs began requiring daily medication. She needed to take the medicine on a full stomach and, rather than shove the pill down her throat, I gave it to her in a piece of cheese. Hoping they might also get cheese, my other dogs sat attentively nearby, and thus our nightly ritual was born.

Sit down and talk to your dog. If you feel strange talking to your dog when other people are around, wait until you are alone. Tell him about your day, or about somebody who made you crazy in traffic. Tell him he is the finest animal on the face of the earth. It doesn't matter what you say; the point is to focus your attention on your dog completely for a few minutes every day.

Find an activity you and your dog both enjoy, and do it. To your dog, life is a team sport. Nothing makes him happier than doing things with you. For you, doing something enjoyable with your dog helps reinforce the feeling that spending time with him is pleasurable. If your dog lives with more than one person, try to come up with different activities for each member of the household.

"What is the hardest thing you ever taught one of your guys to do?" a young man once asked me. I had to consider that for a moment. "Teaching Butch to play football was tough. It took some time for him to grasp the concept of jumping off the offensive line right as the ball was snapped. He tended to wait for his opponent to come to him." The young man chuckled and said, "I'm sorry. By 'guys' I meant your dogs." "Butch *is* a dog," I replied. At that point, my eight-year-old son jumped into the conversation. "See, I play football for my school," he explained. "I wanted someone to practice against at home and Butch loves to jump up, so my mom and I taught him a few moves. Now it's our game."

Activities don't have to be athletic in nature. If you enjoy watching television in the evening and your dog loves to be scratched on the rump, then combine the two—scratch while you watch.

Spend some time face-to-face. At Canine Assistants, we see a huge increase in the bond when new recipients and their dogs spend time face-to-face, connecting on the same level. If you feel comfortable having your dog on the bed or the couch, those are great bonding spots. If you don't, you'll have to meet your dog on the floor for a little face-to-face interaction every day.

While having face-to-face time, eye contact isn't necessary, but a dog who will gaze briefly into your eyes is showing trust. Smile and praise him in a kind voice when he looks at you, to show your appreciation.

We've all heard that you shouldn't stare into a dog's eyes, but staring (as if angry or dominating) and gazing (passively and affectionately) are two entirely different things. If your dog seems uncomfortable with eye contact, don't force the issue. It will get easier as his bond with you increases.

Synchrony. Help your dog learn to synchronize his mood with yours. Begin by teaching him to become excited when you do. This should be easy with most dogs, but some may take a little extra encouragement. Simulate excitement by waving your hands and cheering loudly. After several minutes of acting, suddenly calm down. Completely relax your muscles until your body sags and you let out a big sigh. If your dog does not immediately settle, try closing your eyes. Once he calms for a minute, repeat the excite-relax cycle again. Practice this several times a day, and you will find that when you need peace and quiet, you can settle your dog with merely your sigh.

Last week I was feeling the pressure of having several projects due at the same time, and I began ranting about the stress to my husband. Before he could offer comfort, my two 'doodles, Butch and Jack, jumped up onto the couch with me, both letting out big sighs of relaxation. Before I realized it, I sighed back at them. This is the exact technique I've used many times when I wanted them to relax, so it's difficult to imagine their actions were coincidental. They were bothered about my being so worked up and decided to try a synchronization technique on me. It worked: I felt more relaxed.

Teach your dog to focus on you. Before dogs and recipients graduate at Canine Assistants, we check the strength of the bond that is developing by asking ourselves five questions.

1. How frequently does the dog glance up at his person while they're walking together? We like to see a dog who "checks in" a minimum of once every thirty seconds.

2. When the dog is off-leash in a familiar room indoors, how long before he does a check-in with his owner? A check-in can be returning to the owner physically, but it can also be a quick glance in the owner's direction. Again, well-bonded dogs will check in within thirty seconds of separation.

3. When the dog is off-leash outdoors, how long does it take for him to check in with his owner? We expect it to take longer outdoors than it did indoors, but it still should occur within a minute.

4. When the dog enters an unfamiliar or stressful environment, does he look up at his person for reassurance? We like to see our dogs make frequent check-ins when in a new place or when stressed, such as they might be when at the veterinarian's office.

5. When a treat is placed just out of the dog's reach, does he look to his person for help? Once the dog realizes he cannot reach the treat alone, we like him to look immediately to his human for help or guidance.

The breeds with whom we work at Canine Assistants, such as Labs and goldens, are known for working well with people. If your dog is the independent sort, you can expect him to take more time before making contact, but the test of bonding will still be valid.

HAVE REALISTIC EXPECTATIONS

"He was crazy in the car, pacing and jumping over the seats," she said. "He even chewed on the seat belts. It was a brand-new Lexus SUV. We got it so he could go everywhere with us, but he treated it, and us, with a total lack of respect. It made me upset, but it made my husband furious. To teach him a lesson, my husband threw him out of the car with his leash on, making him run alongside. It made him more stubborn, though, and he started biting us whenever we would try to get the little brat in the car."

That was the story I heard from Frankie's owner in response to my asking why she and her husband were trying to have the handsome yellow Lab euthanized. Frankie was just four months old when they bought him from a breeder. The breeder was located less than ten minutes from the couple's mountain vacation home, but the car trip to their hometown, taken a week later, lasted seven hours. Frankie was calm for the first five of those hours, a remarkable effort on his part. At no point did the owners let Frankie out to relieve himself although they took two bathroom breaks themselves. Frankie was left loose in the vehicle without any toys or any appropriate items on which to chew. After the so-called lesson the couple taught him, his paw pads had to be wrapped for ten days.

From the outset, their expectations of Frankie were so unrealistic that he was doomed to disappoint them. Their reaction to the disappointment was so extreme that the puppy was severely traumatized. Fortunately, Frankie was placed with a new, wonderfully patient owner, but it took many months of gentle encouragement before the young dog could approach a car without fear and apprehension.

If you have realistic expectations of your dog and plan accordingly, your life together will be much easier—for both of you.

Try to see the world through your dog's eyes. Your dog sees the world from the height of a dog, with the eyes of a dog. Those eyes see motion much better than detail and have more acute night vision than humans. Your dog doesn't see colors in the red-green spectrum, but he sees yellows and blues, a wide variety of grays, and through a broader peripheral range.

Your dog's hearing is much more precise than your own. Dogs can hear minuscule changes in pitch and tone. Much of what your voice communicates to your dog comes not from your actual words but from the way in which you say them. Dogs are soothed by calming sounds and potentially overly stimulated by more chaotic ones.

Although he uses his other senses, your dog lives in a world almost exclusively defined by smell. Dogs can distinguish individual odors in a potpourri of scents that people can smell only as a singular whole. Dogs have approximately 220 million scent receptors spread over an area about the size of a Kleenex, while humans have roughly 5 million scent receptors over an area the size of a postage stamp.

Understand that your dog's perspective is quite different from your own. This morning my lovely golden retriever, Nan, had another seizure. Nan reminds me of Princess Grace—blond, beautiful, and composed. Butch and Jack, my male dogs, worship her as the eldest and the only female. But when Nan stumbled over to Jack for reassurance after her seizure this morning, he growled at her. The patience of Job he does not have, but never before has he growled at precious Nan. I was mad at him, but I was wrong.

Poor Jack was simply afraid of Nan in her postictal (after-seizure) fog. He didn't understand what was happening, and I made it worse. In my frustration about Nan's condition, I fussed at Jack for growling at her. Now, in his mind, Nan having a seizure means she will act like a loon and I will be mad at him. I am having one of those days when I'm best described as "all too human."

Clearly, I was expecting Jack to view the situation as I did. Perhaps I was unfairly anthropomorphizing him, but I don't believe attributing human characteristics to him was precisely the issue. The problem was that I had expectations of him comparable to those of an adult human, and no dog ever matures to this level. Jack reacted more in the manner of a young child. Although dogs do not think or feel in the same way people do, we have no choice but to view dogs through our own human filter. Given our limitations, we must be careful not to expect more from our dogs than they are capable of delivering.

Don't scream or hit. All the dogs I have seen in rescue programs who have a history of aggression share one interesting characteristic. On their owner turn-in forms, under "methods of correction used," the owners, without exception, have checked "scream" and "smack." **Aggression leads to aggression—period.** This is true for every breed of dog. There is *no* breed that needs to be handled through yelling, hitting, or any other form of supposed domination. Poor behavior on your part will lead to poor behavior on the part of your dog. It will also destroy your bond more quickly than anything else you could do. If you are angry, walk away. Do anything to keep from taking your anger out on your dog, even if he is the source of your frustration and distress. Remember, your dog is akin to a toddler from another planet. He will simply not comprehend your anger.

"Listen" to your dog. Your dog has the right to provide feedback on his comfort level at any given time, and you have a responsibility to listen and take his feelings into account. Things that are fun for you, such as jogging down a busy, noisy street, might not be fun for your dog. If you want to take him jogging, work with a trainer to help desensitize him, or find a quieter spot for your run. He might hate it when Aunt Martha pats him on the head, or he might not like it when children put their arms around him. **Be his advocate** so he isn't forced to defend himself. Ignoring your dog when he needs you might do irreparable harm to your bond. The more you understand and respect your dog's feelings, the stronger the bond between you.

DOGISMS

In my first book, *Through a Dog's Eyes,* I set down some fundamental truths about the human-dog relationship that I'd come to learn through my years of experience. It's worth repeating them here.

Dogs do not do things solely to anger or frustrate us. They need us too much. Dogs are one of the most successful species the world has ever known. But their survival depends upon our tolerance, so they work hard to keep from displeasing us. They might not always understand what makes us happy, but they never stop trying to figure it out.

Dogs do not speak human. They diligently strive to read our voice tone and body language. Don't expect your dog to leave the steak you just grilled on the counter while you take a shower simply because you say, "Do not eat my steak while I shower." Be clear and reasonable in your expectations of your dog's understanding. (And put the steak out of his reach.)

Rarely does a dog "know better" than to do whatever he is doing at present. When we are tempted to use that phrase, what we really should be saying is, "I know better than to let you do that." Since dogs are much like toddlers, their actions are more a reflection of *our* leadership than *their* character.

Use redirection rather than correction, because it is easier to teach a dog what *to do* than what *not to do*. If your dog is doing something you don't like, show him what you'd prefer he do instead. There are an endless number of things you do not want your dog to use as a chew toy but only a few that you want him to use. Focusing on those few acceptable items makes learning much easier for your dog, and it takes less time and effort. And when your dog is doing the right thing, praise him for it. We all have a tendency to remain quiet until something makes us unhappy. Catch your dog doing something right, and let him know that you're pleased.

Dogs are hyperaware of context. For a dog who learns *Sit* on a yellow carpet, *Sit* means "put your haunches down on yellow carpet." Dogs need to learn behaviors in a variety of contexts before they can generalize the concepts. It takes an average of three exposures in different contexts for a dog to begin generalization. Help your dog understand the meaning of cues by practicing them in as many situations as possible. Be sure your dog learns to generalize the cues given by every member of your household, especially children.

Your dog already knows you are the boss. He needs to learn that you are a leader worth following. I have frequently heard women lament that their family dog listens only to their husband. I suspect in many cases those women aren't making their wishes clear and aren't showing the dog why it is a good idea to do as they ask, using proper reinforcements such as food and toys. Although most men might be doing a good job of encouraging their dogs to follow their directions, I worry that, many times, more masculine voices and more physical handling might make some dogs who are simply scared seem compliant. A dog will not willingly follow a leader of whom he is afraid, and no dog deserves to be frightened into minding his manners.

If you've ever had a lasting relationship with a dog, you know that it's well worth the effort it takes to forge and maintain. A dog's affection is priceless. Nothing beats the feeling of unconditional love directed at you twenty-four hours each day, seven days each week. When you consider that having such an attachment is an integral component of your dog's quest for a good life, it's clear that humans and dogs are perfect partners.

CHAPTER TWELVE

Better Together

Even in his wheelchair, he has the look of a warrior about him. He should. He'd been a soldier in the United States Army for more than half of his life. Then, in less than one half of one second, the time it took for a sniper's bullet to travel three hundred yards, Marcus went from soldier to disabled veteran.

The bullet severed his spinal cord at cervical vertebra 8, leaving Marcus a quadriplegic. In the days that followed his injury, he prayed that his wound would somehow prove fatal, begging God to take him. When it became evident that particular prayer would go unanswered, Marcus began to determine how exactly he would live his life from a motorized wheelchair.

Of all the indignities to which Marcus had to become accustomed, he said that it was his inability to do the very simplest tasks, such as turning on a light switch or picking up the television remote, that left him feeling the most "reduced" (his word). He was not a man who easily accepted help from others.

He applied for a service dog from Canine Assistants to help him do those things he could no longer do for himself. When he met his dog, Kota, his greatest relief was that he could now go many hours without having to utter the words he had come to despise, "Would you please . . . ," to those around him.

About a year after Marcus and Kota graduated, I got an email from him. He reported that all was well. Kota was learning to do additional tasks to help him function more independently. "I knew he'd help me do things, but I didn't realize he would help me handle my injury in more ways than the physical," he confessed. "I really never expected to feel okay about myself again. I thought maybe I would begin to feel less bad, not quite so trapped. But the other day I realized that I'm mostly content with my life now, and I owe the majority of that feeling to Kota."

By *contentment* I believe Marcus meant "ease of mind." I appreciate that particular definition of *contentment* for its flexibility. It can include feeling happy, confident, satisfied, purposeful, or proud. It can mean "without fear, hesitation, or nervousness." It can mean all of those things together—and more. But sustained total contentment would be impossible for either humans or dogs. If our minds remained perpetually at ease, our drives for the necessities of life would be eliminated, and we would not survive. Still, life without contentment in the forefront of our hearts and minds is not a life worth living.

I have always been in awe of dogs' abilities to somehow make those who love them more content, happier, better. Dogs fill a critical need in humans that is impossible to clearly define. It is a phenomenon I see at Canine Assistants almost daily.

Catherine was born with spina bifida, a birth defect in which the spinal column is abnormally formed. She applied for an assistance dog when she was ten years old, but because of our incredibly long waiting list, Catherine didn't receive her dog until she was seventeen. From the day her mom applied on her behalf, Catherine had been enthusiastic about getting a dog, and she handled the long wait with strained patience. She had alternately phoned and written us, or sometimes both, every single month to check on the status of her application. One of the happiest moments of my life at Canine Assistants was calling Catherine to inform her that we'd found a sponsorship for her. Finally, she could come to get her dog. It was one of two times I've known Catherine to be speechless.

Catherine and I had a long talk one afternoon during training camp about our respective philosophies of life. Catherine explained that she was highly driven to succeed and that starting with a disability made her acutely aware that people would have an innate tendency to judge her as weak or incapable. That was unacceptable to Catherine, so she categorically refused to show weakness. This approach had worked well for her, especially academically. She had already received acceptance letters from several Ivy League schools when she came to get her dog.

Emotionally, Catherine was very tightly controlled. She teased her mother, who, much like me, was apt to cry easily and often. Once, during a tearful episode at Canine Assistants, Catherine's mom explained, "These are happy tears." Catherine responded, "Now, there's a concept I just don't understand." "You will one day, I promise," her mother answered wistfully as she stroked Catherine's black hair.

It seemed unlikely that day was going to come while Catherine was at training camp. Indeed, when she was matched with Shaggy, the dog she wanted the most, she expressed her pleasure with only a brief smile. Were it not for the sight of her hand tenderly tickling her dog's ear, I might have been afraid she didn't like him, but I understood her personality.

After the graduation ceremony, Catherine offered only a small, regal wave in my direction as an indication that she and Shaggy were leaving. As she turned into the light, I could see tears glistening on her cheek. A moment after Catherine rolled through the doorway into our parking lot, her mom came back inside holding a small slip of paper. "It's from Catherine," she explained. On the note, written in Catherine's decisive script, were the words, *Happy tears—got the concept.*

· · ·

Dogs help us feel content with our lives and with ourselves. The following letter is from the mother of one of our recent recipients, Channing, about the change in her daughter's ability to handle stress since receiving her dog, Georgie:

> *Hands down by far, stress has been Channing's biggest seizure trigger. Imagine the horror she feels every time a teacher assigns an assignment that will require a presentation to the rest of the class . . . as if speaking in public isn't about the most stressful act on the planet . . . ugh! She's missed class presentations, we've given her drugs (lots of them) to get through the damn thing, she's presented one-on-one to a single teacher, we have been very creative and very frustrated with these in-front-of-the-class presentations. Channing has always had the choice to not present, but that's just one more scenario in life where CG is not normal and she's always striving to be normal.*
>
> *Last week I received an email from Channing's Film Criticism teacher asking what we thought about showing Channing's dog movie to the entire student body at school as part of an official introduction of Lady George (Georgie) the Goldendoodle to the rest of her new classmates, as well as the learning opportunity to find out about others with disabilities. CG didn't even hesitate and said "yes" . . . be still my heart.*
>
> *Rob and I JUST attended the all-school assembly as an on-seizure-call precaution, but low and behold not only was the film shown, but the principal then had Channing and Georgie come up and stand in front of the entire high school and receive a round of applause from over 500 people.*
>
> *Thank you Lady George for giving Channing the confidence and quieting the fear of never knowing when she will have her next seizure . . . this morning was an enormous personal best!!!*

I am often asked what the best thing is that an assistance dog does for his partner. It isn't a difficult question for me to answer. When a dog looks up at a person he loves, he sees that person as absolutely perfect, flawless. To dogs, just like young children, *perfec-*

tion has an entirely different definition than it does for adult humans. Emotion in dogs and young children is not much encumbered by higher intellectual review. It is black-and-white in its nature: "If I love you, you are perfect." When you spend day after day with a dog whose eyes reflect his total adoration, you cannot help but feel more self-confident and content.

Simplicity is peaceful. The more basic our evaluation of what is important, the fewer sources of discontent we have and the easier it is to be happy. "People were animals too once, and when we turned into human beings we gave something up. Being close to animals brings some of it back," wrote scientist Temple Grandin in her book *Animals in Translation*. Human life becomes increasingly complicated as we move further from our natural selves, making contentment harder to reach. Dogs, being thoroughly unimpressed by the convenience of technology, help us refocus on what truly is important.

The very first service dog Canine Assistants placed with a student in junior high school was a black Lab named Toller. He was being placed with a twelve-year-old boy, Calvin, who had Duchenne muscular dystrophy. Calvin and his parents were what my mom would have called salt-of-the-earth people, always polite, kind, and generous nearly to a fault. They lived in a small town and were nervous about the school allowing Toller to accompany Calvin, so I scheduled a meeting with the school's principal.

The family, Calvin included, went with me to the meeting. Over the summer, Calvin had gone from using a walker to using a wheelchair, and consequently he had been struggling socially in school that year. Perhaps it was a combination of the new wheelchair and adolescent angst, but Calvin's classmates, formerly considered his friends, had become his tormentors.

The principal seemed irritated from the moment our meeting began. He reluctantly agreed to allow Toller to accompany Calvin but made it clear that if the dog caused any inconvenience he would be permanently banned from the facility. Then he drummed his pen against his desk in impatience as Calvin's mother tearfully conveyed their concerns about the bullying their son was enduring at the hands of his classmates.

The speed of his pen tapping seemed to increase as Calvin's mom continued, until finally the principal threw up his other hand in a command for silence. Looking straight at Calvin, he said, "Son, the state makes us let you go to school here. Your classmates aren't the ones who are different, you are. You can't expect them to see you the same way, to treat you the same, now that you are so obviously crippled." The principal brought the meeting to an end after his pronouncement. As the family left the room, they thanked the man for his time.

I was speechless with rage over the principal's attitude, though when my speech returned, I used it to have a long talk with the school board. I knew that Toller and his service-dog skills would make life easier both physically and socially in school for Calvin. What kid can resist a dog who knows ninety behaviors on cue? As it turned out, Calvin took Toller with him every day during middle school, and life did improve dramatically. Still, the attitude of the principal rankled in a way I couldn't ignore.

I developed the Canine Assistants Disabilities Awareness Education Program in response to the ignorance of Calvin's principal. Maybe it was too late to change the attitude of adults, but with a cool dog and a room full of children, I felt we could teach the next generation to know better. The plan was to demonstrate the *canine way* of judging the value of an individual.

We now take our service dogs into schools across the country. We talk about dogs, about humanity's relationship with dogs, and then about what assistance dogs are trained to do and why. We choose an individual student to come forward to help. We ask the child three questions: What is your favorite color? Favorite food? Favorite sport? After the child answers, we ask her to sit in a chair and pretend to be quadriplegic. The dog shows off his skills while helping the child with a task she can no longer do as a quadriplegic. Then we ask the child if she is different from the person she was when she first walked up. The answer is, "Yes. I can't move my arms or legs anymore." Then the same questions from earlier are asked again: What is your favorite color? Favorite food? Favorite sport? Inevitably the child repeats her earlier answers. "How can you still like these same things if you are different now?" we inquire. Virtually every child answers the same way: "I'm not different on the inside," beautifully illustrating the point of the exercise.

Finally, we talk about dogs again and how smart they are. Would a dog still love his handler if the handler had eleven heads and seventeen eyes or an arm growing out of her forehead or was not able to see or hear or walk? *"Of course!"* the children shout. How could he? "Because dogs judge people on their hearts and not their bodies," they say. So, we respond, "Do you think we might do better to judge other people on their insides like dogs do?" The presentation ends with the students signing pledge cards, promising to judge people based on what's inside their hearts and not what they look like—just as dogs do.

CHAPTER THIRTEEN

Canine Contentment

Dogs live in a world that is completely controlled by humans, and it's vital that we remember how much their survival depends on our care. We manage their access to food, toys, playmates, sleeping spaces, and virtually all other components of life. If we want to help our dogs reach contentment, we must first examine what makes them feel discontented.

If you return home to find that your dog has torn your house to shreds, you likely have one of two problems. Either your dog is terribly bored and understimulated, or he has separation anxiety. We labor under a disadvantage when working with animals, in that they cannot tell us, at least not verbally, how they feel. However, animals show a more pure response to our treatment, allowing us to reach easier conclusions regarding the efficacy of a particular method and thus the source of the problem. For example, if your dog routinely chews on the door frames when left alone, he might be bored. Then again, he could be suffering from separation anxiety. So if you give your dog something to do while you are gone and you return home to find that he hasn't been chewing door frames, boredom was likely

the cause of his destructive behavior. If you give your dog something to occupy his time while you are out and he still chews the
woodwork, separation anxiety is the more probable source.

BOREDOM

Boredom is an enormous source of stress for dogs. They desperately
need something to do, both physically and mentally. Physical stimulation requires getting your dog "panting tired" at some point every
day. Daily exercise is not just a fun activity for your dog but a tiring
one as well, reducing his energy levels and, in turn, inappropriate
behavior. In addition, it's important to challenge your dog's brain
every day. Although excellent "thinking" toys are available for dogs,
the best mental stimulation is learning new behaviors and vocabulary words. Chaser, a border collie from South Carolina, is known
as the smartest dog in the world, with a vocabulary of more than a
thousand words. I'm currently working with a rescue dog named
Einstein on vocabulary, with amazing results. Dogs love using their
remarkable brains just as much as their athletic bodies.

To help with boredom, put away your dog's food bowl. Canids
in the wild spend approximately 80 percent of their waking hours
searching for food. Putting your dog's kibble in a bowl could be a
waste of resources and opportunity. You might already be using
some of your dog's daily ration as behavior rewards, but you can use
the remaining portion as great boredom busters.

I mix a portion of my dogs' daily kibble into low-fat cottage
cheese and pour the mixture into a hollow toy, such as a Kong. I
freeze the stuffed toy overnight, pulling it out in the morning when
I leave for work. The frozen mixture can take hours for even large
dogs, such as my 'doodles, to lick clean. Puzzle-type toys, which
challenge your dog to figure out how to get the kibble, can also be
great entertainment. If you have more than one dog and do not
crate them while you're away, you might need to secure toys in different rooms of the house so that the dogs won't argue over who
gets which. I run a length of light chain through the middle of hol-

low toys before filling them, so that I can clip them to eyehooks I have placed unobtrusively around the house.

Be careful not to leave your dog alone with any toy he can tear apart. Fleece or squeaky items are for play only when you're available to supervise. Remember that novelty is what makes toys exciting, so rotate the playthings available to your dog. The absence of a particular toy for a few days makes a dog want it even more.

Doggy day care is a fantastic idea for a dog who is young and healthy. As an added benefit, day care is usually an effective way to manage separation anxiety. Your dog plays while you work, and you both go home tired. Compare this to dragging home from a long day at the office and being met by your sweet dog who has been waiting all day for you to come home and play. Even if you are able to be home during the day, doggy day care can still be a great exercise and socialization source. Just be careful about the day-care facility's approach to handling the dogs. Dogs should be separated by size and activity level.

Asking a doggy day-care facility how they handle growling dogs will tell you all you need to know about their dog sense. Management techniques such as squirting water in a dog's face whenever he is growling at another dog are dangerous and can be counterproductive. Many people assume that if a growling dog is squirted with water, according to the principles of *operant conditioning* he will be less likely to repeat the behavior in the future. What they fail to understand is that *classical conditioning* is taking place at the same time. So what actually happens is that the punished dog increases his negative feelings toward the dog at whom he was growling. In other words, the very sight of that dog now predicts in your dog's mind that something bad is going to happen.

Dog walkers can also be a great resource for exercise and bathroom breaks if your dog has to spend long periods alone. Professional dog walkers should be bonded for your security, and remember to carefully check references for anyone you hire.

One of the best ways to prevent boredom—and bad habits such as excessive barking that can develop or be exacerbated when a dog is bored—is to give your dog jobs around the house. Appendix G illustrates how to teach your dog to tug and retrieve. Once he has learned those skills, you can give him various household chores. Teach your dog to put away his own toys, place laundry in the hamper, and even hunt for items you frequently mislay, such as car keys. Hardworking dogs are happy dogs.

That is most certainly the case at Canine Assistants. For our dogs, it's as if work is a form of play, for which they get copious praise and multiple treat rewards. It also helps that our teaching method, Choice Teaching, allows the dogs a sense of control, so tasks do not feel compulsory, merely the best course of action. The ability to control, or at least influence, one's own environment is a significant source of contentment for all living beings.

SEPARATION ANXIETY

In addition to alleviating boredom, choice also helps reduce the feelings of helplessness that may result in separation anxiety. Social animals, including dogs and humans, need social contact. People held in isolation often report making friends with spiders or mice, creatures of whom they'd normally be afraid. Simply stated, social isolation is terrifying for social animals.

Social attachment is necessary for survival, so our brains are wired to feel social separation in ways that cannot be ignored. Neurobiologists call the emotion of social isolation *panic*. The area in the brain that controls social attachment is extremely close in proximity to those areas that manage pain; determine our attachment to certain environments, such as our homes; and regulate body temperature. This is evident in our language; hence when we lose someone we love, we say, "It hurts" or "I feel lost without him." We describe people with whom we might form attachments in terms of temperature, such as "She's a cold fish" or "She has a warm heart."

As wired as dogs are for social contact, it is somewhat surprising that they do not suffer more serious separation anxiety. After all, dogs remain emotionally akin to toddlers the entirety of their lives, particularly in terms of their inability to survive on their own. Being left alone must be frightening to someone who cannot be told or fully comprehend the concept that you will return.

Although other animals can sometimes help with separation anxiety, it is not foolproof, so be careful about obtaining one animal in an effort to comfort another. It is more likely that you will end up with two animals who panic when you are gone. Likewise, crating or confining dogs who have separation anxiety can be counterproductive. Panicked dogs can hurt themselves attempting to escape from confinement.

Separation anxiety can be especially difficult to treat, so you should seek professional help, preferably from a veterinary behaviorist, if your dog is experiencing anything more than mild distress. Medication will likely be combined with behavior modification in a treatment plan. Most dogs who have separation anxiety do not get better without medication. Brain chemistry can make it impossible to treat problems such as this with a single modification protocol. Be sure you give the medication exactly as prescribed, allowing it enough time to begin working. Recording exactly what your dog does, rather than how you think he feels, can be helpful in these situations. Many times improvement takes place in slight increments, so changes can be easy to overlook without precise record-keeping.

Until you can get your dog's condition under control, you must formulate a plan to avoid leaving him alone. I realize this might not be easy, but if you do not accept the responsibility, every time he's alone and afraid his fear will be reinforced. You can use day care, a friend, or a relative to watch your dog while you're away.

Changing your behavior can help prevent the development of separation anxiety and even work as a treatment for those dogs with mild symptoms. Start by teaching him how to be alone according to the guidelines listed in Appendix H. Never make a big deal out of leaving or returning. Leave your dog something yummy that he gets only while you are out of the house, such as a Kong stuffed with steak and cheese. Hand him the special treat as you leave and take it away the second you come in the door. Soon he will be packing your briefcase for you.

Many trainers and behaviorists believe that management techniques such as not allowing a dog who has separation anxiety to solicit your affection or sleep with you are effective steps to reducing the problem. Some even advise ignoring your dog completely for five to ten minutes upon returning home. I strongly disagree. A dog who gets an abundance of affection is more apt to develop the confidence needed to stay alone. For many years, child-development specialists encouraged forcing needy children to spend time apart from the primary objects of their attachment. Most have now reversed their positions based on studies that suggest children who spend more time close to their parents show increased confidence when left alone versus children who are denied parental attention. So if you have what is known as a "Velcro dog," one who seeks your constant attention, giving him what he craves will help him require less attention from you over time.

SUPERSTITIONS

The little dog named Suzy had grown up in the city. The sound of honking horns and urban chaos was her norm. Suzy's guardian, as she always called herself, was a petite older woman named Alice. Together they shared an apartment with Alice's son, Hunt, and daughter-in-law, Alison.

One day in late May, while out walking Suzy, Alice had a massive stroke, dying on the sidewalk as her dog lay next to her. Naturally her son was called to the hospital, so a neighbor took charge of Suzy when the ambulance arrived and kept her until the son was able to return home.

Hunt was afraid that Suzy had been so traumatized by the incident that she would never want to go walking again. However, Suzy was resilient and thoroughly housebroken, so she continued to stroll the neighborhood streets on her leash. Several months went by, and her new routine was well established. Then one day as Suzy was being walked, she suddenly began panicking, pulling on her leash and panting heavily, snarling, and snapping at seemingly nothing. About thirty seconds later, she stopped as suddenly as she had begun.

This behavior recurred nearly every day thereafter, but only on her morning walk. Hunt took Suzy to the veterinarian, but no physical cause could be found. Finally, at the recommendation of a mutual friend, he called me. He told me the story of his mother's death and Suzy's new behavior. I asked him to videotape, for two consecutive days, the strange conduct and everything that was happening around them at the time.

In the footage from both days, I could see several people and vehicles. My immediate thought was that Suzy had been so traumatized by her mother's sudden death that she had developed a superstitious association with something or someone she was now seeing on her morning walks. What I could not figure out was why it had taken nearly three months for the behavior to begin. For days I watched the footage and contemplated what might be Suzy's undoing. Finally it struck me. Alice had died in late May. Suzy's panic attacks began in early September. In the video from each day, a school bus appeared. Hunt did some investigating and discovered that the bus had been on the street at the time of his mother's stroke. As it turned out, Alice had died on the last day of the school year, so Suzy hadn't seen the bus again until the following September.

To Suzy, the presence of the school bus meant death. Once we figured it out, her superstition was understandable to Hunt and Alison. They began walking her after school had started each day, and she never had another panic attack.

Suzy's reaction to the school bus is an excellent example of why traumatic punishment in dogs often does not work as intended. Dogs associate what happens with whatever their senses register at the moment it occurs. This is understandable when you consider that dogs do not have representational language. When you think about what happened to you yesterday, you likely narrate it in your mind with words. Scientists used to believe that verbal language is what gave humans intelligence and consciousness and, therefore, animals were assumed to be without awareness, intellect, and emotion. If a dog screamed in pain, it was considered a purely reflexive behavior. That simply is not true. What is true is that animals process information differently than do humans. Because animals don't have words, they must store their memories in other ways. Animals think in sensory memories: pictures, audio clips, and whiffs of scent. If a dog receives a painful leash correction just as another dog walks past, the sensory memory associated with the passing of another dog is likely to be a feeling of pain.

Once a dog has developed a superstitious fear, the memory of it is permanent. That does not mean you cannot change his behavioral response to the memory, but it does mean that you might have to be exceedingly patient. You might also need help. These post-traumatic-stress–type fears are serious, and treating them might require you to find a trainer who has experience with such issues. If typical counterconditioning and desensitization techniques do not work, be prepared to ask your vet for a referral to a veterinary behaviorist.

THUNDERSTORM PHOBIA

Phobias are essentially irrational fears or irrational responses to legitimate fears. Some individuals develop a phobia of specific items, such as clowns or balloons, that most would consider harmless. Others develop exaggerated fears of occurrences that are potentially harmful, such as storms. These fears are not irrational in themselves, because there is indeed a possible threat, but the extent of the exaggerated response becomes abnormal.

Thunderstorms can be frightening. In addition, they have the potential to cause serious damage and bodily injury. Nevertheless, few of us dig into our bathtubs, pant, pace, and even jump through windows when confronted by a thunderstorm. However, some of our dogs do. A dog in the unrelenting grip of true storm phobia is about as far from a contented creature as you could possibly imagine.

No one knows for sure what causes thunderstorm phobia in dogs. Some scientists believe that it is a change in barometric pressure. Others contend that it's the sound of thunder or the sight of lightning. Still others believe that dogs are reacting to the increase in static electricity and the potential for electric shock. Certainly, it could be that different dogs are reacting to different components of the storm. Or it could be a combination of things that frightens dogs. Until they can tell us, it is impossible to know for sure.

Dogs who grow up in the kennels at Canine Assistants do not have a fear of thunderstorms. I have not witnessed a single case in the more than twelve hundred dogs who have lived with us on the farm. Because we have cameras monitoring each kennel, I've had the opportunity to watch hundreds of hours of real-time video of our dogs during storms, and not once have I seen them take any notice at all, unless startled by a particularly loud clap of thunder or a close lightning strike.

That said, we have had dogs who've developed a fear of thunderstorms once they graduated and left our facility. This leads me to believe that it is the condition of the housing at Canine Assistants that makes the difference. While on our farm, the dogs live in groups, providing constant social companionship for one another. It is possible that our dogs keep one another calm. Studies have indicated that the presence of another dog can have a calming influence on the one who is storm-phobic.

Static shock seems to be extremely upsetting for many dogs. Unpredictable static shock, as dogs often experience when storms are present, appears to make some dogs completely crazy. Because our kennels are made of concrete, which does not conduct static electricity, it is likely that our dogs are protected from this experience.

But then, unpredictable shock would make most animals nuts. So in an effort to understand why random shocks would have such a profound effect on the behavior and emotions of most dogs, I attempted an experiment. I placed one of the latest-model shock collars around my own neck and asked a friend to treat me as if I were a dog in training. She selected certain behaviors, unknown to me, that she wanted me to perform and others that she wanted me to avoid. If I did one of the undesired behaviors, I was to receive a mild shock in correction.

Although I had tested shock collars on my arm, something about having one around my neck made me uncomfortable. When

I received a shock for the first time, I froze, afraid to move. Then I panicked, anticipating that standing still might cause me to receive another shock. Finally, I began moving cautiously around the room, but when the second shock came unexpectedly, I lost it. I fell to the floor. Although the shocks didn't hurt, it was not knowing when they would come that sent me to my knees. It created a primal fear in me that's difficult to convey, and I tore my fingernails in the rush to get the collar off my neck. Although this experiment speaks to the absurdity of shock collars as training tools, it also demonstrates the fear that can be created by static formed unpredictably during storms.

Many dogs have similar feelings about the prospects of being zapped without knowing how to prevent it. The majority of dogs who are fearful of thunderstorms dig in places such as bathrooms, where there is typically no carpet or furniture to conduct electricity. This is likely an effort to reduce the random static shocks.

Dogs who are fearful of storms cannot control their behavior, so being frustrated or angry with them is futile (not to mention mean). Dogs who panic and lose complete control need medication before they can be helped behaviorally. Speak to your vet about what medication might help your dog calm down enough to respond to behavior-modification techniques.

Additionally, if your dog has only a modest thunderstorm phobia or is already on medication for calming, I suggest a nonstatic body wrap. Bundling him in it before the storm begins can further reduce his anxiety. This treatment utilizes both the well-documented calming effect of swaddling combined with the static guard to keep your dog safe from future shocks. A study by Dr. Nicholas Dodman, published in 2009 in the *Applied Animal Behaviour Science,* asserts a reduction in stress in storm-phobic dogs using this method.

Music, such as that which comes with the thoughtful book *Through a Dog's Ear,* can also have a calming effect. Some people have reported success with homeopathic remedies in mild cases. Desensitization using sound tapes has been anecdotally reported as helpful, but I have not had much success with them. Thunder seems to be the Pavlov's bell of storms, signaling something bad is coming, but it appears that the sound alone is not enough to produce a fear response in most dogs. However, if it is for your dog, you might try using a recording of storms to help him slowly grow accustomed to the noise. Start at a very low volume, one your dog can tolerate without stress, and slowly increase it over time. Provide your dog with other positive associations such as treats and toys as you let him listen.

It is okay to cuddle a fearful dog. Recent studies show that when a dog is in the grip of a true phobia, your petting him will not do harm and might give comfort during the episode. Do not allow panic or concern to come through in your voice; always keep your tone upbeat.

One of my friends throws a party for her dogs when a storm is coming. They eat yummy food, listen to music, and play ball, and it seems to have reduced her dogs' anxiety about thunderstorms. It is a great technique to use with dogs who are uneasy but not completely panicked.

Phobias are treatable. Do not give up on your dog simply because he is afraid of something you might not understand. Get help from trainers and veterinarians to deal with his fears. It's heartbreaking to see the number of dogs turned in to shelters every spring because they are afraid of storms. This should never happen.

When I watch the YouTube video entitled "Earl at work - Goldendoodle" posted by one of our Canine Assistants recipients and see the expression on the big dog's face or when I read the following poem written in honor of Becca and her service dog Kringle, I am reminded that dogs who are allowed to do what they love, for those they love, are the happiest dogs on Earth.

To Love Her

Every creature that is wise enough to obey the inner voice,
The inner voice that calls and directs and points to the path
Has a divine purpose, a reason to live
My purpose is the only thing I know
My purpose is to love her

Maybe her voice has been inside me all my life
It must be so
Because she is all I know
I do not merely follow *her*
As though I have no choice but to tag along
Rather, I walk beside *her*
Because I choose to follow the voice that leads me
My purpose is to love her
She is my soul mate, my partner
My purpose is to love her

ROBBI VAN SCHOICK

All sentient beings need purpose. Handling your dog's stressors is the first step on the path to contentment. The second step is determining what gives your dog purpose and then allowing him to do it. If your dog loves to retrieve, teach him to bring you the newspaper each day. If his inner clock never runs late, teach him to wake the children up for school every morning. If he lives to announce the presence of guests to your home, teach him to alert you by nudging your hand when someone approaches the door.

Sometimes, in order to suit your dog's particular passions, you may have to be creative in developing a "job." If he loves to dig, allocate him a small place in your yard and bury treasures for him to dig up. If you don't have a yard, buy a plastic tub, bury the treasures in shredded newspapers, and keep it in your kitchen.

If the only purpose you can see in your dog's life is that his existence makes yours happier, remember that he is performing the most precious service of all . . . and value him accordingly.

CHAPTER FOURTEEN

Reason Enough

Shannon Mitchell watched the cars ahead of her on Georgia 400 swerve to the left to avoid something in the road in the far right lane. She couldn't tell what it was, but she hoped it wasn't an animal who had been hit. It was only six A.M., and she was already late for work. The last thing she needed this morning was to see something sad. As she drew closer, she detected a slight movement. "Damn," she thought aloud. It was definitely an animal—maybe a bear cub. It seemed to be trying to cover something with its body. All thoughts of being late flew out of her head as she edged her Honda Accord toward the right shoulder of the road.

It wasn't a bear cub. It was a dog, a large Newfoundland. The dog had wrapped itself protectively around another dog, this one a golden retriever. The golden was clearly injured, most likely hit by a passing car: the fur on his chest and abdomen was matted with blood. As Shannon approached, the Newfie looked at her and began whimpering.

Another motorist stopped, and together they were able to slide the injured golden onto a blanket that Shannon had in her car. The big Newfie supervised the entire process, and once the golden was settled on Shannon's backseat, he crawled carefully into the car himself, resting on the floor. Shannon raced the golden to a nearby veterinary clinic, where he was found to have several deep gashes and a broken pelvis. But overall he was in remarkably good shape. The Newfoundland stayed quietly, though emphatically, beside his friend while he was examined. To be cautious, the vet suggested that the golden stay in the clinic for the day so they could keep an eye on him. The Newfie stayed, too.

When all attempts to find the owner of the two big dogs failed, Shannon adopted them both. She named the golden Sam and the Newfoundland Shadow. Sam and Shadow remain the best of friends, though their adventures are now confined to safely fenced areas.

Dogs are remarkably loyal to those they love, and they don't love just members of their own species. Amazingly, they love us as well.

The story running on the television at the Atlanta airport was about the recent landslides caused by flooding near Rio de Janiero. As the piece neared its conclusion, the camera panned across the devastation and stopped on a shot of a medium-sized dog lying in the mud near a small wooden cross. The reporter explained that the dog had refused to move for the past two days, despite continued enticement from the relief workers. The cross, he explained, marked the grave of her owner, who had been killed in the landslide.

Tears were pouring down my face by the conclusion of the story. I was embarrassed to be weeping in the middle of the busy airport, until I noticed the distinguished gentleman seated just to my right surreptitiously wiping his eyes with the back of his hand.

Later that week, I was doing an interview about assistance dogs for a magazine. The reporter and I had been discussing dogs who alert their human partners to oncoming seizures.

"Why do they do it?" she asked.

At first I misunderstood her question and began detailing my theory that the dogs who can anticipate the onset of seizures were picking up on some scent-based marker, so slight as to be undetectable to humans.

"No, no. I meant, why do they bother?" she interrupted.

"Because they care about us," I answered. "For whatever wondrous, unfathomable reason."

"Is there a more cynical reason others might suggest?" she asked.

"Well, some people say dogs only care about the people who feed them, that theirs is a purely selfish motivation. We all have to do what is in own our best interest in order to survive, so I am certain that argument is partially correct," I noted. "It would be for people as well. But dogs' affection toward man goes far beyond that. I am not sure that we will ever understand the *why* of it completely."

As people, we are driven to understand all the whys. It is our nature to question kindness, to look for the selfish motives behind selfless acts. Sometimes in dogs, the only discernible motive is kindness itself.

Several weeks ago, I was speaking with a neurologist acquaintance of mine about the value of dogs for people with epilepsy. He was clearly a believer in their special abilities and had an obvious passion for dogs. When he relayed his story, I understood why.

In 1920, a baby girl named Heddy was born into a large Jewish family in Czechoslovakia. When she was six years old, her parents moved the family from their small town nestled in the Carpathian Mountains to a larger town where opportunities were more plentiful. At that time in Eastern Europe, secondary schooling was the exclusive right of males, so Heddy took an apprenticeship with a wig maker when she was twelve years old. Although eighteen months younger than she, the wig maker's son fell in love with Heddy. As the years went by, the age difference between the two began to matter less, and Heddy found herself returning the young man's affections. In 1939, concerned about events in Nazi Germany, the two decided to marry and emigrate to Palestine. The rabbi in their community was not as concerned about Hitler as he was about the couple's youth, and urged them to put their plan on hold and wait a few more years before marrying. They hesitantly agreed.

The young couple was right to be worried. Under the Nazi occupation a year later, the wig maker's son was sent to a forced-labor camp. And in the spring of 1944, Heddy and her family were sent to Auschwitz.

Although most of her family were immediately executed at the camp, Josef Mengele himself decided that Heddy, her two sisters, and one cousin were strong enough to be used as laborers. They were sent to one of the large wooden barns where the female workers were kept. The barn provided little in the way of comfort. The floors were strewn with hay that functioned as both bedding and bathroom. There were large gaps between the boards that formed the sides of the barn, which afforded the women some fresh air but also left them at the mercy of the elements.

Every day, the women were forced to dig deep holes along the roads leading into the camp. They then had to cover the holes with tree limbs and other debris in the hopes that the approaching Russian tanks would fall into the holes and stall. The women were worked hard, fed poorly, and allowed only minimal rest. Those who couldn't keep up were shot in front of the others as a warning.

The day came when Heddy, hampered by a chronic leg injury, was threatened with death. That night she told her two sisters, her cousin, and six other women that she was going to try to escape. They agreed to go with her. Russian troops could be heard in the distance, and the women knew they would be safe if they could reach them.

While the other six women ran under the cover of darkness, Heddy, her sisters, and her cousin decided to hide under the straw in the barn until the German soldiers stopped searching for them; then they would run. When morning came, the SS officers called roll as they usually did and discovered that ten young women were missing. They immediately called for the search dogs and set out tracking the escapees. The six women who had fled the previous night were quickly found. Guards returned them to the barn, lined them up against the wall, and shot them. Then they took the dogs back outside to continue searching for the other four.

Heddy, still hidden under the hay, could hear the German shepherds sniffing along the side of the barn, and she held her breath, praying that she would not be discovered. Suddenly, one of the dogs stuck its head in between the slats directly in front of Heddy. The frightened woman and the dog looked at each other directly, eye to eye. Suddenly the shepherd turned away, as if it had found nothing, and resumed sniffing.

After the guards left the area, the women slipped into the woods and made their way to the Russian lines. They had successfully escaped. Not long after, Heddy was reunited with her young man, who remarkably had also made a successful escape from another camp. They married and ultimately moved to Phoenix, Arizona. They had children, one of whom was the neurologist telling me this story, and always, rounding out the family, a German shepherd.

His mother was absolutely certain that the German shepherd at Auschwitz knew what was at stake: If it did its job and alerted its handler to the presence of the women, the women would be killed. She believed that the dog risked its own life to protect the lives of the four women.

Dogs care about people. The *why* of it is irrelevant.

For years, Canine Assistants has conducted the K9 Kids Reading Program. Elementary-school students who are struggling to read at grade level practice by reading aloud to our dogs. The children seem to love having the dogs as classroom partners, claiming that their time with a book in their hand and a dog's head in their lap was the most fun part of the day. Improved test scores have repeatedly demonstrated that the program is as effective as it is enjoyable.

One day a Canine Assistants volunteer took Tobias, a puppy just six months old, to an elementary school to participate in K9 Kids. Not long after they arrived in the first-grade classroom, the school's tornado siren sounded. This was not a drill, and the children knew it. The kids were instructed to sit in the hallway and place their arms over their heads.

The siren was very loud, and Tobias was clearly frightened by it until he noticed a little boy crying at the far end of the hallway. Tobias tugged hard at his leash, straining to reach the child. The volunteer asked the boy if he would mind Tobias sitting with him. The child readily agreed, and instantly the puppy began licking the little boy's tears, his own fear completely forgotten.

When the tornado warning expired without incident, the children were led back into their classroom. As the little boy handed the leash back to the volunteer, he kissed the top of the pup's head and whispered softly in his ear, "Thanks."

Dogs make our lives happier, healthier, and safer. They make us smarter and more patient. They afford us the kind of peace and contentment only the natural world makes possible. When we provide for them, we are providing for ourselves. When we fail them, we fail ourselves.

While on the book tour for *Through a Dog's Eyes,* I heard many tragic stories about dogs who had been mistreated or misunderstood. In Kentucky, a woman in her late thirties told me about her dog, Galahad. Galahad was a smooth-coat collie who loved the four children with whom he lived. He also adored their mom, Beth, who taught fourth grade at the local elementary school. But Galahad's very best friend was their dad, Grant.

Grant worked at home, so he and Galahad were together almost all the time. They went on walks nearly every day, and Galahad spent his afternoons under Grant's desk, lying at his feet. All was wonderful in the household until the awful day that Grant died suddenly of a heart attack. From that moment on, the previously quiet and well-mannered Galahad changed. He stopped eating and began having accidents in the house. He tore Grant's favorite chair to shreds. He howled and barked day after day, until finally the neighbors begged Beth to do something.

Beth was beside herself. First she had lost her husband; now her dog had suddenly gone nuts. Not knowing where else to turn, she called local dog trainers for help. The first trainer she hired suggested putting a collar on Galahad that would shock him whenever he made a noise. Beth couldn't bear to do that, so she engaged another trainer. But this one also suggested a shock collar, the type that Beth could trigger herself, allowing her to correct Galahad for barking or any other behavior she found unacceptable. Again, this was something Beth simply could not do. Finally, although reeling from the money she'd already spent on trainers whose advice she couldn't take, Beth turned to the best-known trainer in her area, paying him five hundred dollars for a two-hour consultation.

This trainer, a locally famous disciple of the Dog Whisperer, told Beth that, in his professional opinion, since her husband's death Galahad had taken over as the alpha in the family. He advised Beth that if she truly cared about the dog, she would do whatever it took to break his spirit. Though Beth loved having Galahad sleep in her now otherwise empty bed, as he had done when Grant was alive, the trainer was emphatic that Galahad needed to be crated in the basement overnight. The trainer showed Beth other techniques for reinforcing in Galahad's mind that she was the alpha. Although Beth tried, she could not do them well; her heart was not in it. She couldn't get past the feeling that Galahad was desperately missing Grant. The trainer was forceful: If Beth could not do better, she should consider whether or not she was "emotionally strong enough" for Galahad. Perhaps she should give him away to someone more capable of handling him. Beth was devastated. Galahad was her link to Grant, and she didn't want to lose him, so she tried to follow the trainer's advice.

A friend, aware of her difficulties, gave Beth a copy of my book *Through a Dog's Eyes*. As she read, Beth realized that her instincts were correct: Galahad was heartbroken, not misbehaving. He was expressing his sorrow the only way he could. Suddenly the solution seemed clear. When Galahad would howl, she would comfort him. They would snuggle on the couch or in the bed and, as Beth put it, "cry together."

At last report, Galahad and the rest of the family were doing better. They had adopted a kitten who worshiped Galahad, following him around like a duckling behind Mama duck. Beth said she knew Galahad still missed Grant, as they all did, but now he was eating and back to being the bed hog he had always been before Grant died.

I honestly believe that Cesar Millan is oblivious to the damage he has done in the world of dogs and thus in the world at large. I cannot imagine he ever intended to do harm. I think he cares a great deal about dogs and it would break his heart if he ever understood the gravity of what he has unleashed. Of course, not all of what he preaches is inappropriate. What he suggests about the need for exercise and time together is fantastic. But, the show-the-dog-who's-boss approach he espouses is incredibly dangerous. It is not a great distance on the continuum from thinking it's acceptable, in fact advisable, to be physically rough with a dog, to out-and-out abuse. Cruelty is cruelty; the form it takes is merely a matter of degree.

The appeal of dominating dogs, particularly large, powerful ones, seems to cut across every socioeconomic boundary. Aggression toward living beings can be a self-reinforcing behavior. For many, it feels good to release anger as aggression. Your body gets a massive adrenaline rush, creating a high, and the behavior becomes difficult to control. Psychologists who study and counsel on domestic abuse contend that the treatment for people who abuse other living beings is extremely complex because of the addictive nature of the rush that comes from aggression. Abusers get better at abuse, increasing their need for greater and greater adrenaline surges and necessitating more deviant behavior. Over time, they move further up the ladder from animals to children to women.

VULNERABILITY

I remember holding my dog Nicholas and weeping as I read a *New York Times* article my friend sent me about Alex the parrot and his caregiver, Dr. Irene Pepperberg. As I related in my first book, Dr. Pepperberg wanted to work with a nonprimate who had the ability to vocalize, in an effort to better understand how animals think and feel. Alex, who died suddenly in 2007, was highly intelligent.

But it wasn't what Alex thought that moved me so. Rather, it was what Alex felt, displaying clear and intense emotions that would rival those of humans. Alex would get angry with Dr. Pepperberg. He would also apologize. Once, when he had to be left overnight in a veterinary clinic, Alex called out to Dr. Pepperberg, begging her not to leave him, using *please, I'm sorry,* and *I love you* in context and with emotion.

Alex did not, in reality, feel contrite when he said, "I'm sorry," but he did feel sad and afraid. Dr. Pepperberg placed his emotional capacity at about the level of a two-year-old child's. The point is that Alex, with a brain the size of a walnut, was a sentient being. Brain size and intelligence do not have a one-to-one correlation, and Dr. Pepperberg's findings have stunning implications for our dogs. Alex allowed me to understand that dogs are cognitively capable of a great deal more than previously recognized. And as such it is morally wrong not to respect their feelings.

ALL WE NEED TO KNOW

In 1789, the English philosopher Jeremy Bentham wrote, "The question is not, Can they reason? nor, Can they talk? but, Can they suffer?" In 2011, we know that our dogs don't experience merely physical suffering but emotional pain as well, and it is this knowledge that compels us to redefine appropriate treatment. They are not simply *dogs* in the way that label has traditionally been used. Dogs are thinking, feeling creatures, and no amount of comparative analysis to humans or cultural tradition can make acceptable the abuse of those who suffer.

We must remember that our dogs are not wolves. They are both our wards and our teammates, but never our enemies. Our relationship compensates for our individual weaknesses as species and creates a whole vastly superior to the sum of its parts.

What do dogs want? They want a good life. What do dogs need in order to have a good life? They need the care, concern, affection, and benevolent guidance of people. Why should we care about dogs? We should care about dogs because they don't just *need* us in their lives, they *want* us in their lives. Anyone who has ever known the love of a good dog understands that that alone is reason enough.

The couple had been married for almost a year. The husband, Daniel, was a stockbroker; his wife, Jenna, was doing her medical residency in obstetrics. These highly intelligent, successful people were furious with a thirty-six-pound puppy named Carlo. They believed Carlo was deliberately provoking them. He wasn't. He was a nervous puppy doing his best to communicate with people who were essentially deaf to him. Carlo gave off good signals; the couple simply didn't respond appropriately.

The first tip I gave them was, "When the puppy growls at you, stop doing what you're doing, and then he won't be forced to bite you."

The wife nodded in understanding, but the husband went nuts over this piece of advice. "I am not having a dog dictate the house rules to me!" he shouted.

"I understand completely. You shouldn't let the dog dictate the rules, but he is already doing that by biting you when you upset him," I explained. "In order to fix this, we need to change his feelings about those things that are distressing him. Then, once emotion isn't clouding Carlo's judgment, we can explain the rules to him in a way he can understand."

"What would fix this is my drop-kicking him across the floor the next time he tries to bite me, but I know my wife would never forgive me if I did that." Daniel's hands were tightly clenched as he spoke. It was clear that he felt Jenna was keeping him from "handling" the situation.

I spent an hour trying to explain to Daniel that engaging in a battle with Carlo wouldn't be a fair fight—it would be bullying. It's precisely what bothers me most about the alpha model and similar methods. These models assume dogs are dumb animals until a problem arises, at which point dogs suddenly become worthy opponents who must be defeated.

One of my favorite Canine Assistants supporters often shows his concern for me by exclaiming: "I am for you!" I love this. In a world that seems to embrace the idea of *You are either for me or against me,* he's declaring himself to be on my side, and that provides great comfort.

Our dogs are always on our team. Always. They place no conditions on their attachment. It is one of the very best parts of dogness. It is what allows them to forgive us our transgressions and always remain clearly on our side. It's called loyalty.

Driving home from Carlo's house, I was depressed. I hadn't gotten through to Daniel. I began contemplating the concept of dog *guardianship* versus *ownership,* wondering if those who proclaim we have no right to own companion animals were correct in their assessment. I couldn't imagine life without dogs, cats, and horses. I didn't want to believe that it is unfair to keep companion animals, but I couldn't shake the feeling that maybe I should . . . for their sakes. I was in a dark mood when I got home—that is, until I opened my email and found a letter about a little dog named Oliver.

While visiting my in-laws, I had met a woman who told me that her daughter had adopted one of the dogs from Michael Vick's kennel. The woman was kind enough to share her daughter's phone number. I was hesitant to call, feeling certain Oliver's mom had fended off more than her fair share of media requests. It was enough for me to know that Oliver was well and truly loved.

Then, several months ago, I read an essay entitled "Lessons Learned: Acting as Guardian/Special Master in the Bad Newz Kennels Case," written by Rebecca Huss, a professor at Valparaiso University School of Law. I was reading a section about Ms. Huss and Tim Racer, an advisor skilled with pit bulls, visiting Vick's dogs in order to make the best possible decision on the fate of each. These paragraphs, written by Ms. Huss, were especially poignant to me:

During my visits I obtained information that was unavailable through regular reporting. For example, one dog, Oliver, appeared quite withdrawn and stressed during the first evaluation in September. He was not responsive to the various stimuli used during the evaluation. Although Oliver did not show aggression toward humans, he appeared extremely fearful of people. When Racer and I approached Oliver, he crouched down against the wall of his upper tier kennel and watched us closely. I began to wonder whether it was fair to keep Oliver alive when he was so clearly miserable. The September evaluation results were very discouraging, and it was unclear how many more months Oliver would be required to stay at the shelter. One of the animal control officers was assisting us in taking out each dog, and Racer and I told her that we did not want to stress Oliver by trying to remove him from the kennel. She then told us that when she cleaned his cage, he would place himself against her body. This showed that Oliver may have had a chance of appropriately living and interacting with humans. Racer removed Oliver out of his kennel, and Racer and I sat with him for quite some time.

Specifically, there were two aspects of Oliver's behavior that Racer noted that might indicate Oliver's ability to bond with people given the right circumstances. The first is that when Oliver was allowed to roam on his own in a large enclosed area he would periodically "check back in with us"—circling back towards us and trotting over our legs even though at that point he was free to stay away from us. The second indication was that when Racer or I would hold Oliver closely, Oliver's body would relax against ours.

Oliver's case is a clear example of why my visiting the dogs was so important. If the animal control officer did not mention her interaction with Oliver, I may have decided it would be more humane to recommend he be euthanized. Because I looked beyond the reports, Oliver was placed with Best Friends Animal Society and is making progress in his recovery.

I assumed this was the same Oliver about whom I'd heard from his human grandmother. Suddenly I felt an urgent need to call Oliver's mom. I promised myself I would be as unassuming as possible, simply wanting to verify again that the dog was safe, that he had made it.

I needn't have worried about intruding. Oliver's owner, Erika, welcomed my call as if she'd known me forever. She asked only that I give her time to seek permission from the appropriate sources before sharing Oliver's story with me.

When I didn't hear anything for several weeks, I began to think I wouldn't be learning the details. One morning several weeks later there was an email in my inbox from Erika.

I remember it like it was yesterday. It was toward the end of July 2009, and I was getting ready for work. I saw on the news that Michael Vick was eligible to play football. I was absolutely livid. I had already decided that Karma would take care of him and what he did to those innocent victims, but this particular news tossed my inner peace clean out the window. For days, I was just plain angry. I yelled at everyone who crossed my path, my vision blurred, I screamed at nothing, you name it. I have always allowed things to just "roll off" my back as normally whatever is bothering me is out of my control . . . Then I realized something—I wasn't going to let Vick ruin me! I decided to take matters into my own hands and adopt one of his victims . . . I chose to take all my extremely negative energy and channel it into love and adopt one of Vick's victims. I have been a member of Best Friends for years, and I had followed the story of the Vick victims they took to their sanctuary. I contacted the adoption man-

ager at Best Friends and told her what I wanted to do. And the process started.

My husband, David, and I had to jump through several hoops to even be considered to adopt one of these dogs. Then, we had to have a local representative from Best Friends come to our home and conduct a home visit. We visited, answered questions, and the rep watched how David and I interacted with Boss (our 128-lb. shepherd/husky mix). We passed our "home visit" with flying colors! The adoption paperwork was finalized and we passed a criminal background check. The next step was to make a trip to Utah with Boss for a meet-and-greet with one of the Vick victims to see how we all got along. Best Friends chose Oliver as a match for our family. IT WAS LOVE AT FIRST SIGHT!!!! I have never, ever been more excited in my life than I was the morning we got the notification that we were approved for the adoption. It was October 2009 when my husband checked email and saw we were approved. He woke me up and told me the great news, as he knew how much I wanted this dream to come true.

We had to wait a couple of weeks and Oliver had to be hand delivered to our doorstep by a Best Friends trainer, Tamara . . . When Tamara pulled up in the driveway with Oliver, I could barely contain myself! MY BABY WAS FINALLY HOME!!!! I have never been more excited! I rushed out to the driveway and opened the van door and showered Oliver with kisses and hugs. I didn't want to let go of him!

Our next step was to find a trainer who was certified to train Oliver and me so that Oliver could pass his Canine Good Citizenship (CGC) test. Per the courts, Oliver was technically in our foster care until he passed his CGC. If Oliver didn't pass his CGC within three months, he could have been taken away from us. The pressure was on!

The day that Oliver arrived home, the local trainer showed up to spend the day with us and to meet Oliver. We started training immediately. Oliver came home the weekend before Thanksgiving of 2009. At first, we trained almost every day with the trainer, and then Oliver and I worked together one-on-one. We *attended our weekly classes, and in February 2010, Oliver passed his CGC!!! I was so, so, so, so, so very proud of Oliver. The local trainer was excellent! She put her heart and soul into training both Oliver AND me! She was as excited to be a part of this as I was!*

Oliver's foster mom from Best Friends told me that Oliver very rarely came out of his crate, as this was his "safe place." I asked her about kisses, as I love to kiss animals and have them kiss me back. Oliver started sleeping in bed with Boss, Squeaky (our cat), David, and me the very first night he came home. He now "rules" the bed! Oliver started by "bumping" my face with his nose—this was his way of kissing me. Now, he showers me with kisses every single night and every single morning. I remember the day Oliver first kissed me. It was about 6:15 A.M. while I was getting ready for work. I called my husband, my mom, and even one of my bosses at home yelling, "OLIVER KISSED ME! OLIVER KISSED ME!"

You know, after all that kid had been through, I cannot believe he allowed himself to trust us! I wouldn't trust people if I had been through what he had been through. He saw things that NO ONE should EVER have to see! He heard things that NO ONE should EVER have to hear! He heard his "friends" screaming as they were beaten, shot, drowned, electrocuted, and thrown to the ground like someone using the dogs for a jump rope and pounding their bodies to the ground. I was informed that Oliver was used as a bait dog. His teeth were filed down. He has some nerve damage in his ear (one won't stand up at all), and he has some nerve damage in his mouth. He eats fine, but food falls out of the side of his mouth when he eats.

He has minimal scarring on the outside. His damage is mainly psychological, but even that is healing. Boss has been a great role model for Oliver. He now loves to run and play with Boss and Squeaky. He loves to curl up in my lap. He is full of energy and love.

To be able to give Oliver a fresh, new start and a fresh, new life is the proudest moment in my entire life! I truly cannot say

*enough about how much I love Oliver and how extremely grateful
I am that he is a part of our lives. Every night when we retire to
bed, Oliver kisses me and I kiss him back and I tell him, "I'm so
proud of you and I'm so glad you are home."*

When I told Erika that she was a hero, she insisted that Oliver
was the real hero. I think there is ample room on the pedestal for
both of them.

Erika showed me that the best of humankind is nothing short of
extraordinary. She gave me hope that by example we can perhaps
give people such as Daniel a better understanding of animals. To
understand dogs is to realize they deserve our respect and compassion.

Companion animals exist . . . we sent that train out of the station a long time ago. As a concept, companion animals will go on
without our help; as individuals, they will suffer without our inter-
cession. Our companion animals can live good lives with us. Our
dogs—all dogs—deserve good lives. Miraculously for us, they want
us beside them as they go.

Appendices

Veterinary Emergencies

Remember that before working with any injured dog, you should muzzle him. Wounded animals lash out and, as cruel as it seems to muzzle a hurting dog, you will not be able to help him if you are on the way to the hospital yourself. Many dogs will reflexively grab your hand or arm with their mouths in an effort to say, "Stop, that hurts!" Unfortunately, our skin is no match for canine teeth, even when they are being used merely to indicate extreme discomfort.

The goal of muzzling is not to tie the dog's mouth completely shut, but rather to keep him from opening it wide enough to bite. Tying the dog's mouth too tightly might cause additional stress and anxiety and should be avoided. Using a long piece of fabric, such as a leash, necktie, or pantyhose, make a loop and knot it. Place the loop over the dog's muzzle with the knot under his jaw and tighten it snugly. Drawing both free ends back around the dog's neck, tie a shoelace bow. In essence, you are making a figure eight with his muzzle through one loop and his neck through the other. The tied muzzle loop keeps the dog from opening his mouth fully and the neck loop ensures he will not remove it with his paws.

SHOCK

When a dog's circulatory system cannot adequately supply oxygen to body tissues, a generalized depression of the entire body occurs, as organs attempt to function under less than ideal conditions. This failure to oxygenate and the resulting changes associated with organ malfunction is known as shock. In veterinary medicine, trauma is the most common cause, but others could include infection, burns, hemorrhage, and heart failure. Dogs in shock have pale gums, rapid heart rates, and weak pulses. They might be noticeably cold, weak, and mentally unaware of what is going on around them. In some cases, the dog might be completely unconscious.

Successful treatment of shock requires immediate veterinary attention in order to diagnose the cause and to administer appropriate care. As you prepare to transport your dog to the veterinarian, you should first muzzle him and quickly assess obvious injuries, such as bleeding or fractures. Try to keep the dog immobilized by using a board or sling when moving him. Wrap the dog in towels, blankets, or garments to conserve body heat and prevent further decline. Drive safely.

HIT WITH FORCE

Any time a dog has been hit by a car, been kicked by a much larger animal, fallen from a high place, or in any other way been struck with force, it should be considered a true veterinary emergency. If the dog is unable to stand, do your best to come up with a backboard of some type before moving the dog. Although a solid surface like plywood would be ideal, you can use a blanket or tightly stretched towel if you have other people to help you. Gently roll the dog onto your backboard and transport him to a vehicle. Getting to a veterinarian is of primary importance in these cases because of the potential for internal injuries.

BLEEDING

If your dog is bleeding, your first goal is to stop the flow of blood. If the wound is severe and the blood is spurting or really profuse, press clean gauze or cloth against it and maintain pressure *while* you get the dog to a veterinarian. Don't peer under your bandage— merely hold it steady. If the wound is not bleeding at an alarming rate, press clean gauze or cloth over the wound for a minimum of three minutes (time it if possible) before you check to see if it is clotted. Most of us keep checking every few seconds, and that can often reopen the wound. If the wound is not clotting after three minutes and there is a significant amount of blood, reapply the pressure and get to a veterinary clinic.

Try to find someone who can drive you so that you can maintain pressure on the wound. If a profusely bleeding wound is on a leg, you can try a tourniquet of cloth *tightly* wrapped between the wound and the dog's body. Loosen the tourniquet for twenty seconds every fifteen minutes and reapply. If a wound is severe enough to require a tourniquet, it is definitely a veterinary emergency, and you should head immediately to your nearest clinic.

Not all bleeding will be obvious; for example, internal bleeding can result from blunt force trauma, such as being hit by a car. Internal bleeding might result in pale gums and a slowed CRT, as you would expect with shock. Monitor a dog's gum color and CRT to assess for shock and the severity of blood loss. You should head immediately to your veterinarian if the dog's gums become paler than usual.

BURNS

If your dog gets burned, apply an ice-water compress to the area. If the burn is deep or larger than the size of a quarter, your dog needs to be seen by a veterinarian. If not, the best treatment we've found at Canine Assistants for burns is a liberal application of regular table honey to the area once a day. Lightly wrap the wound so that the dog cannot lick the honey off. Honey provides all the nutrients needed by healing tissue and has antimicrobial properties, helping to prevent infection. When you remove the bandage, gently clean the burn with soap and water to remove the yellowish film. This film is the remnants of the honey and not infection. Simply clean, reapply the honey, and rebandage the area daily until the wound has closed.

CHOKING

If your dog appears to be choking but is able to breathe, look in his mouth with a flashlight. If you can see the obstruction, use pliers or tongs to try to grab it. Be careful not to push the object farther down the airway. You can also turn smaller dogs upside-down to see if gravity might help dislodge the object. If the object isn't easily removed, it is best to get to your closest veterinary clinic.

If your dog cannot breathe, stand behind him and position him in a semi-upright position. Place your left fist just under the point in the center of his chest where his ribs come together, put your right hand over your left, and give a firm thrust back toward his backbone and upward. Repeat until the object dislodges or you have a ride to the nearest veterinary clinic, at which point you should switch to the technique below.

If you cannot get your dog into an upright position or you are transporting him in a car, lay him on his side, put both palms on his rib cage, and press firmly three or four times. Repeat until you get to a veterinarian or the object dislodges.

NOT BREATHING/NO HEARTBEAT

When a dog isn't breathing, you should first tilt his head slightly upward. Then open his mouth and gently pull his tongue forward until it is flat. Using a flashlight, check his throat for the presence of a foreign body. If you can see an obstruction, follow the steps for choking. If you can't see anything, begin rescue breathing immediately. Close your dog's mouth and breath into his nostrils until you see his chest rise. Then briefly release his mouth to allow for exhalation. Repeat this sequence every four to five seconds. The best-case scenario here is that you do resuscitation efforts in the back of the car that is driving you and your dog to the nearest vet.

If you are unable to raise his chest and it feels like the air is not going in, possibly there is a foreign object that you cannot see. In such cases, treat as described under "Choking" to dislodge the obstruction.

As you are doing your rescue breaths, use your free hand to check for a heartbeat. If you cannot do both, give him four breaths before checking for a pulse. Your dog's pulse can best be felt by placing your index and middle fingers as high up as possible on the inside of his leg, approximately where his leg meets his body. Move your fingers toward the point halfway between the front and back of the leg. Here you should feel a slight recess, where the blood vessels run. Keep your touch light, as pressure will make it impossible to feel pulsing. If your dog has a pulse, continue rescue breathing as before while heading for the nearest veterinarian. If your dog doesn't have a pulse, roll him on his right side. His heart is in the lower half of his chest on the left, just behind his elbow. With palms down, place one hand on top of the other and begin compressions of approximately two inches. You should continue at a rate of two compressions per second for a medium-sized dog. Go slightly slower for a larger dog and slightly faster for a small dog.

Do not perform rescue breathing and compressions at the same time. Do ten compressions and then give a rescue breath. Repeat the sequence until the dog begins to recover or you reach veterinary help. If you are able to reestablish a heartbeat, it is often necessary to continue providing rescue breaths, because spontaneous breathing is slower to return.

The current recommendation in human emergency medicine is to begin chest compressions after checking the mouth and calling 911. The goal is to provide one hundred chest compressions per minute without providing any breaths, because deep compressions draw air into the lungs. These guidelines have not yet been adopted for dogs, to my knowledge, although it seems logical that if you are unable to provide breathing, simply do chest compressions as quickly as possible until help arrives.

HEATSTROKE

In warm weather, if your dog lies down, becomes unwilling to move, experiences vomiting or diarrhea, and is panting heavily, you might need to initiate treatment for heatstroke. Take his rectal temperature to determine whether your dog is experiencing heatstroke. Typical rectal temperatures during heatstroke are greater than 106°F. Using tepid—*not cold*—water or alcohol, wet gauze or towels and place them over his armpits, groin area, and paw pads. Do not waste much time trying to treat this at home. Heatstroke is a true veterinary emergency. Intravenous fluids, oxygen, medications, and other treatments may be necessary.

SEIZURES

Seizures are normally not life-threatening emergencies, but they are terrifying to watch. Know that your dog isn't aware of what is happening and isn't frightened. The best thing you can do for a seizing dog is to check your watch when the seizure begins (they usually last approximately two to three minutes), then clear the area around the dog so that he will not be hurt by objects in his path. Don't try to restrain him or place anything in his mouth. If the seizure lasts longer than four minutes (four minutes seems endlessly long when it is your dog who is seizing, so do not guess if at all possible), call your veterinarian for directions. If a seizure ends in less than four minutes, you still need to check with your veterinarian, but the matter isn't urgent. Postictal behavior in dogs is almost more difficult to watch than the seizure itself.

Many dogs seem afraid and act goofy for hours after a seizure. You may certainly comfort your dog now. Lack of coordination is also common during the postictal phase, so don't panic if your dog staggers or bumps into things. If after some time your dog begins a second seizure, you need to take him to your veterinarian for evaluation and treatment with a drug such as Valium to stop future seizing. There are many causes of seizures, and multiple events might indicate a cause other than epilepsy such as cardiac, metabolic, or neurologic disease.

The good news is that, thanks to the research being done by pharmaceutical companies such as UCB (makers of the human antiseizure medications Vimpat and Keppra), more treatments are becoming available for people and dogs who have seizures.

FRACTURES

If you believe your dog has a broken bone, get veterinary help as soon as possible. If you can see the break, take him to the vet immediately. Dogs who can ambulate on three legs can usually be allowed to walk to the car and later into the veterinary hospital. It is sometimes helpful to support older dogs through the use of a towel sling placed under their chest or abdomen. If he is unable to ambulate, it is best to transfer the dog to a board or stretcher for transport. If your dog has an open or compound fracture, cover the area with a light gauze bandage to control bleeding and prevent contamination. Be sure you have a muzzle in place before attempting to cover the wound. In the majority of cases, attempts by owners to splint a fractured leg serve only to enhance the dog's pain and the owner's odds of being bitten. Everyone is much better served when the injured dog is moved to a board, placed in the car, and taken quickly to a veterinary hospital.

BLOAT

Gastric dilatation and volvulus (GDV), commonly known as bloat, is always a veterinary emergency. There is nothing you can do to treat it yourself, and when left untreated it is always fatal. Though dogs of any size and activity level can bloat, the classic scenario is a giant- or large-breed male gobbles his food, tanks some water, and then runs outside to romp in the yard. His stomach is bloated with air that he swallowed while sucking down dinner and begins to bounce as the dog plays. The mix of food, water, air, and play creates a perfect storm in which the stomach flips over and twists like a wrung-out bath towel. In addition to being extremely painful, the twisting of the stomach and small intestines causes blood to pool, and the dog begins to exhibit signs of shock.

Common signs of GDV are retching, severe pain, inability to rise, depression, and a distended abdomen. As shock and pain progress, the gums become pale or bluish, the skin feels cold, and the heartbeat becomes more difficult to find. Transport the dog to the nearest veterinary hospital immediately before shock develops further. In all likelihood, surgery will be required on a dog experiencing some level of shock. The sooner you arrive at your veterinarian's, the better your dog's chances for survival.

EYE AND EYELID INJURIES

Common emergencies involving eyes include scratches to the cornea, foreign bodies in the eye, eyelid lacerations, and proptosis (the dislocation of the eye from the eye socket, which requires immediate care to preserve sight).

- Scratches to the surface of the cornea are very painful and will require daily medication. Dogs with corneal abrasions typically squint or keep their eye shut and may rub their face repeatedly with their front paw. Excessive watering will be obvious. A moist compress might provide some relief until your veterinarian can examine your dog.
- Foreign bodies in the eye can be treated by flushing the eye with water or, preferably, contact solution. Do not attempt to remove an object from the eye or eyelids if you cannot flush it out.
- Eyelid lacerations are not as painful as injuries to the eye itself; however, it is very important to have the eyelid sutured to preserve normal function. When left to heal without surgical closure, the eyelid will not be able to maintain an adequate tear film over the eye, and a chronic dry-eye condition may occur.

- Proptosis is most common in breeds with flattened faces and bulging eyes, such as pugs. Do not try to replace the eye or pull the eyelid back over the eye. Keep the eye moist with a wet cloth, K-Y jelly, or contact solution while driving to the veterinary clinic.

Common Household Toxins

The following list, though it contains many of the household toxins to which dogs can be exposed, isn't complete. Call the Animal Poison Control Center (888-426-4435) for substances not on the list. As previously noted, there is a small charge for contacting the center, but it's well worth the cost if you are in an emergency situation.

- apples
- apricots
- cherries
- peaches
- plums
- **grapes**
- onions
- **raisins**
- nutmeg
- **xylitol (sugar substitute)**

- yeast dough
- alcohol
- **chocolate**
- mushrooms
- macadamia nuts
- tulip bulbs
- hyacinth bulbs
- daffodil bulbs
- sago palm
- peace lilies
- Easter cactus

- crown of thorns
- azaleas
- crocuses
- rhododendrons
- tiger lilies
- clematis
- foxglove
- lily-of-the-valley
- narcissus
- morning glories
- **antifreeze**

- cocoa mulch
- **some chemicals, such as fertilizers and weed killers, used on lawns and gardens**
- **poisons used to kill rodents**
- certain cleaning products
- **human medications, such as Tylenol**

(Note: Those items in boldface are particularly dangerous to dogs.)

Desensitization and Counterconditioning for Dogs Exhibiting Specific-Object Guarding

Note: You must give your dog a treat during each repetition of these exercises. Break treats into small pieces or use his kibble for all exercises except those marked with an asterisk. On those steps, give him a *fantastic* treat, such as six slivers of thinly sliced chicken or roast beef. (We call these jackpots.) The exercises will not be easy, but we want him to develop highly positive memories of relinquishing objects when asked to do so.

If at any point your dog growls or seems uncomfortable, back up a step and proceed more slowly. We do not want him growling through any of these exercises.

GENERAL RESOURCE GUARDING

Step 1: Toss your dog an object with which he has no guarding history, from a distance of five feet. Approach him and retrieve the object. As you do so, pull a treat from your pocket with your other hand and give it to him. Immediately after giving him the treat, return the object and walk away. Repeat this drill from various angles.

Step 2: Now approach your dog from ten feet away and retrieve an unguarded object. As you do so, pull a treat from your pocket with your other hand and give it to him. Immediately after giving him the treat, return the object and walk away. Repeat this drill from various angles.

Step 3: Approach your dog from twenty feet away and pick up the unguarded object. As you do so, pull a treat from your pocket with your other hand and give it to him. Immediately after giving him the treat, return the object and walk away. Repeat this approach from various angles.

Step 4: From a distance of six feet, toss the unguarded object to the dog. Approach him and stroke him lightly on the back for two seconds. Then pick up the object, hand him a treat with the opposite hand, and return the object. Repeat this approach from various angles.

Step 5: Repeat step 4 but increase the stroking time to five seconds.

★Step 6: Leash your dog and tether him to a solid, stationary object. Sit down several feet out of your dog's reach. Put an object your dog has guarded in the past just out of his reach. Pick up the item, toss the dog a treat with your other hand, and put the item back down. Repeat several times. If he guards at all, increase your distance until he isn't guarding, then slowly decrease the distance.

Step 7: Keeping your dog tethered, hand him the item without letting go. Offer him a treat with your other hand as you take the item away.

Step 8: This time, let go of the item for half a second before taking it back. Next try two seconds, then five seconds, then ten seconds.

★Step 9: Let the item go, stand up, bend over, and immediately remove the item.

Step 10: Hand your dog the item, back up ten feet, then approach him and take the item.

Step 11: Hand the dog the item, back up ten feet, and wait there for five seconds before approaching and taking the item. Increase the wait time by five seconds each trial until you have reached thirty seconds.

Step 12: Hand your dog the item, back up twenty-five feet, then approach and take the item.

Step 13: Hand your dog the item, back up twenty-five feet, and wait there for five seconds before approaching and taking the item. Increase the wait time by five seconds until you reach thirty seconds.

Step 14: Hand your dog the item, and leave the room for five seconds before approaching and removing the item. Increase the length of your absence by five seconds up to thirty seconds.

★Step 15: Stash the item where the dog can reach it while on his tether. As soon as he grabs the item, approach and take it.

Step 16: Repeat as above, but leave the room for increasing intervals of five seconds up to thirty seconds before returning and claiming the item. When you reach thirty seconds, jump to two minutes.

★Step 17: Untether the dog and repeat steps 15 and 16 while he is off-leash. Block tables and all other places he can "den," but otherwise let him go where he chooses.

For extra practice, repeat steps 6–17 with a rawhide roll.

The steps can be done one day at a time or more quickly, depending on your dog's behavior and your schedule. If there is any chance your dog will bite you over anything in the process, get expert help immediately.

FOOD-BOWL GUARDING

(Desensitization and counterconditioning schedule for dogs who have a low bite risk)

Notes:

- A "tidbit" is a very small piece of something *yummy*, such as roast beef or chicken, that the dog usually does not get.
- If at any point the dog appears stressed or threatens you in any way, slowly back away and stop for the day. The following day, begin again at the last stage tolerated by the dog.
- All these exercises must be done when the dog is full from a recent meal, unless otherwise noted.

If the dog is not comfortable with your approaching his empty bowl when he is full (has recently eaten a normal meal), get a new bowl and place it in a *new* location.

Stage 1: Approach the empty bowl from a distance of six to ten feet, and drop a few tidbits in it for the dog to eat. Repeat this from different angles and at different gaits (faster, slower, etc.).

Stage 2: Approach the empty bowl from twenty feet away or more, and drop a few tidbits in it for the dog to eat. Repeat this from different angles and at different gaits (faster, slower, etc.).

Stage 3: Approach the empty bowl from six feet away, and bend over slightly while dropping tidbits into the bowl.

Stage 4: Approach the empty bowl from ten feet away, and bend over slightly while dropping tidbits into the bowl.

Stage 5: Approach from six feet away and bend at the knees, reaching down with your tidbit hand as if to grab the bowl but stopping short of actually touching it. Pause for a count of three, and then drop tidbits into the bowl.

Stage 6: Approach from different distances and angles and at different gaits. Bend at the knees and extend your tidbit hand as if to grab the bowl, but stop short of actually touching it. Pause for a count of three, and then drop tidbits into the bowl.

Stage 7: Approach from ten feet away, and touch the bowl for a split second with the hand that is *not* holding tidbits. Then drop tidbits into the bowl.

Stage 8: Approach from different distances and angles and at different gaits, and touch the bowl for a brief second with the hand that is *not* holding tidbits. Then drop tidbits into the bowl.

Stage 9: Approach the bowl from ten feet away, and touch it with the hand that is *not* holding tidbits, for a count of three. Then drop tidbits into the bowl.

Stage 10: Approach the bowl from different distances and angles and using different gaits, and touch the bowl with the hand that is *not* holding treats, for a count of three. Then drop tidbits into the bowl.

Stage 11: Approach the bowl from ten feet away, and move it around with the hand that is *not* holding tidbits, for a count of five. Then drop tidbits into the bowl.

Stage 12: Approach the bowl from different distances and angles using different gaits, and move the bowl around with the hand that is *not* holding treats, for a count of five. Then drop tidbits into the bowl.

Stage 13: Approach from a distance of ten feet away, and pick up the bowl with the hand that is *not* holding tidbits. Drop tidbits in from the other hand and replace the bowl onto the floor.

Stage 14: Approach from various distances and angles and at various gaits, and pick up the bowl with the hand that is *not* holding tidbits. Drop tidbits in from the other hand, and replace the bowl onto the floor.

Stage 15: Approach from ten feet away, and stroke the dog lightly on the back as you are dropping tidbits into the bowl.

Stage 16: Approach the dog from different distances and angles and at varying gaits, and stroke the dog lightly on the back as you are dropping tidbits into the bowl.

Stage 17: Approach the dog from ten feet away, and stroke the dog on the back for a count of five before you drop tidbits into the bowl.

Stage 18: Approach the dog from different distances and angles and at varying gaits, and stroke the dog on the back for a count of five before you drop tidbits into the bowl.

Stage 19: Approach the dog from ten feet away, and pick up the bowl. Hold the bowl in your tidbits hand, and stroke the dog lightly with the other hand for a count of five, before dropping tidbits into the bowl and replacing the bowl on the floor.

Stage 20: Approach the dog from different distances and angles and at varying gaits, and pick up the bowl. Hold the bowl in your tidbits hand, and stroke the dog lightly with the other hand for a count of five, before dropping tidbits into the bowl and replacing the bowl on the floor.

Once you have made it through all of these steps with an empty bowl, repeat them with a bowl of kibble.

Teaching the Gentle Mouth to an Adult Dog

When dogs have not learned bite inhibition as puppies, their bite can cut even when they're only playing. Although I'm not certain that it's possible to teach true bite inhibition to an adult dog, it is relatively easy to teach him to have a gentle mouth.

My favorite way to teach a dog to be gentle is to feed him his kibble one piece at a time with my fingertips. It's a relatively simple process. Start by holding a piece of kibble between your index finger and thumb, saying "gentle" as you let your dog sniff and nibble at the food. Say the word *gentle* in a slow, drawn-out manner (imitate a Southern drawl). You always want cue words to sound similar to the actions they request, so a request to be gentle should be said in a relaxed and mild manner.

If your dog is too rough, say, "Uh-oh," and put the kibble back in the bowl or in your pocket. You want him to understand that if he is rough, the food goes away. Your definition of *too rough* should become more demanding as your dog gets better at "gentle."

Once your dog is calm and gentle when taking kibble, you

should repeat the exercise with a treat your dog especially loves, such as a small piece of bacon.

I also like having a toy with which my dog can be rough. This toy can be tugged, shaken, thrown, or whatever else the dog wants to do. When he's playing with this toy, I bring out another toy, one that I've designated "baby." The dog can only sniff and lick "baby"; he is *never* to treat it roughly. If he gets forceful, I remind him with "gentle."

I practice *gentle* at least once a month, even with Butch, who is well traveled and highly social and has great bite inhibition.

The Super Dog Protocol

These five exercises provide a puppy unique neurological stimulation from day 3 to day 17 of his life. Do them no more than once per day and for only five seconds each, because overstimulating a puppy this young can have harmful, rather than beneficial, effects.

1. Tactile stimulation: Hold the puppy in one hand, and gently tickle him between the toes on any foot, using a Q-tip.

2. Head up: Using both hands, hold the puppy perpendicular to the ground (keeping his body straight) for five seconds.

3. Head down: Holding the pup firmly with both hands, point his head toward the ground for five seconds.

4. Supine position: Hold the pup so that his back is resting in the palm of both hands, with his muzzle facing the ceiling, for five seconds.

5. Thermal stimulation: Use a damp towel that has been cooled in a refrigerator for at least five minutes. Place the pup feet-down on the towel for five seconds, and allow him to move freely.

Studies have shown that dogs who did Super Dog as pups have

- improved cardiovascular performance (heart rate)
- stronger heartbeats
- stronger adrenal glands
- more tolerance to stress
- greater resistance to disease

Some studies also indicate that Super Dog gives puppies greater self-confidence and an increased capacity for learning, even as adults.

Socialization Checklist

Although some highly neotenized breeds, such as the Cavalier King Charles spaniels, likely have a slightly longer socialization period, most experts agree that the socialization window closes for puppies somewhere around twelve weeks of age. Before that period has passed, puppies should have at least one positive experience with each of the following.

- babies
- crying babies
- toddlers
- loud toddlers
- children
- playing children
- teenagers
- men of as many ethnicities as possible
- women of as many ethnicities as possible
- men with hats and beards
- men carrying packages

- men who have deep voices
- women wearing hats
- women wearing flowing skirts
- joggers
- people in uniform
- people who wear glasses
- people wearing raincoats
- people using umbrellas
- people using wheelchairs, canes, and crutches
- clapping
- people knocking at the door
- doorbells
- shouting
- helium balloons
- busy streets
- crowded parking lots
- groomers
- a veterinary clinic
- a boarding kennel
- parks (although if other dogs are present, keep your pup in your arms, because he isn't fully immunized)
- playgrounds
- cats
- a select few well-mannered, well-vaccinated dogs of various sizes
- anything else your dog might see in his daily life with you

Note: There is a fear period for many puppies at around eight weeks of age. Be sure that you do not let your puppy get scared during his socialization. If he seems fearful of particular stimuli, retreat and allow him to gradually acclimate himself.

Teaching the Tug and Retrieve

TUG

Tugging is a great interactive game. Studies show that dogs who play tug with their owners pay more attention to them. At Canine Assistants, our dogs win the tug-a-war far more often than they lose. The idea that an owner should never let a dog win while tugging is ridiculous. Games are meant to build confidence. It wouldn't be much fun for your dog if he always lost! The exception to this is that your dog must *always* release the item when you ask him to "give." Start by holding a treat in the other hand to offer as an incentive for him to "give." You should be able to quickly eliminate the treat. Be careful not to let your dog get so excited about tugging that he forgets his manners. If you feel out of control at any point, ask him to "give," and quit the game. If he will not let go, be totally still, and he eventually will. Tug can be played vigorously, but it must always be played politely.

If your dog will not tug at all, try this tip. Put several small treats in the center of a bandanna, then wrap a rubber band around the middle to create a pouch of treats. Keep another few treat pieces hidden in your hand. Hold the bandanna where your dog can smell it easily, then lift it over his head so that he must stretch a bit. If he touches the bandanna with his mouth, drop it and one of the treats hidden in your hand as you say, "*Yes,* good tug," such that he believes it was the act of pulling on the bandanna that dislodged the treat. Slowly increase the amount of pressure you require before releasing the bandanna and a treat. Once he is tugging well, add the cue *Tug* as you move the bandanna over his head. Once your dog sees that tugging can be really fun, treats should no longer be necessary, because the game itself will be his reward.

RETRIEVE

Choose a canvas-covered retrieving dummy that is the appropriate size for your dog. If you can't find one small enough or you want to save a little money, you can easily make your own by buying a yard of canvas and a small bag of firm stuffing. Simply cut the canvas to the appropriate width (about two-and-a-half times the width of your dog's muzzle), insert enough stuffing to make the roll about one-fifth the width of your strip, and roll the strip snuggly over the stuffing. Tie both ends of the roll tightly with string, and you're done. Retrieving dummies work well because they do not encourage dogs to bite down hard, which could undo some of your bite-inhibition work.

If your dog is a natural retriever, you do not need this section. If he retrieves without returning the item, skip to step 10.

Pick a time when your dog seems to be naturally active. For many dogs, this is early morning and early evening.

Step 1: Start by waving the dummy in front of your dog and tossing it just a few feet away. We are going to do this in stages. Initially, we care only about moving toward the toy; it doesn't matter if he will not touch it or bring it back right now. If he shows no interest in the dummy, find a toy, any toy (even a slender rawhide), that he does like. Use his preferred toy until he is comfortable with each step, at which time you should again try the dummy.

Step 2: Once he consistently goes toward the toy, begin saying "Go" as you toss the item. Now as your dog approaches the toy say, "*yes,*" and give him a highly desirable treat.

Step 3: Toss the item, say "Go," and then walk toward the item with your dog. Wiggle the item until he touches it with his mouth. When he does so, say, "*yes,*" and give him a highly desirable treat.

Step 4: Once your dog consistently touches the toy while you wiggle it, begin adding the phrase *Get it*. As soon as he does, say "*yes,*" and give him a highly desirable treat.

Step 5: Continue directing your dog to "go" and "get it," but slowly decrease the amount you wiggle the toy; then, even more slowly, begin removing your hand from the toy altogether. Taking your hand away from the toy makes this a whole new deal in your dog's mind, so be patient. You may repeat your *Get it* cue if necessary. Make your dog successful even if it means you have to wiggle the toy a bit or put your hand back on it; he'll get it eventually. The first time your dog puts his mouth on the toy without your hand touching it, you should throw a party! Give him a happy "*yes*" and a small handful of highly desirable treats.

Step 6: Now you are going to stop tossing the item and begin holding it in your hand for your dog to take. Ask him to "get it" as you hold the item at his eye level. You might have to wiggle it a bit at first, but you should quickly be able to wean him away from movement. As soon he has the toy in his mouth, *gently* stroke him under the chin while saying "Hold it." Have him "hold it" for a count of two at first, and slowly work up from there. After the appropriate count, place your hand on the toy and ask your dog to "give." As soon as he releases the toy, say, "*yes,*" and give him his yummy treat.

Step 7: Once your dog can "get it" and "hold it" for a count of twelve while your hand is at his eye level, begin moving the toy toward the ground. Move approximately two inches closer to the ground after each successful repetition. Once the toy is on the ground, slowly remove your hand. Remember, this is the hard part, so be patient. When your dog does "get it" from the ground without your hand touching the item, throw another party and give him multiple pieces of treat.

Step 8: Now that your dog can "get it," "hold it," and "give," you can begin tossing the toy. Start by tossing it a foot from you. Say "Go" as you release the item, then "Get it" as he reaches for it, and "Hold it" once the item is in his mouth. Now say "Give" as you step toward him. If he drops it before you reach him, say "Uh-oh," and begin again.

Step 9: Once your dog returns the retrieved item consistently, begin backing up as he moves toward you. Don't go far; you only need to help him understand that he has to get the item to you before you will say "*yes*" and give him a treat.

Step 10: Now begin increasing the distance you toss the item. By this time, you should have a dog who is more than willing to retrieve what you throw.

Desensitization Schedule for Mild Separation Anxiety

Desensitizing a dog who has mild separation anxiety focuses on reducing his dependence on your constant presence and reducing the intensity level of your arrivals and departures. Progress will be slow, so be patient.

Your starting point will be based on your dog's tolerance. You want to keep him sub-threshold (not in a state of worry), so if your dog can tolerate more, skip step 1.

Step 1: Try feeding your dog his kibble lightly mixed with peanut butter, or squirt cheese into a Kong-type toy, placing it in the room where your dog stays when you leave. Block the room so that he cannot leave, but remove yourself from his vision. If he panics when you are out of sight, immediately return and stay with him the first day. On subsequent days, increase the amount of time you stay out of sight by ten-second intervals until you reach two minutes.

Step 2: Once your dog tolerates your absence for two minutes, you can increase your absences in two-minute intervals until you reach ten minutes.

Step 3: Once your dog tolerates your absence for ten minutes, increase your absences by ten minutes until you reach one hour. At this point, you should add an additional treat of high value, such as another Kong-type toy stuffed with a mixture of low-fat cottage cheese studded with small pieces of bacon. As soon as you return, you must pick up the treat. Your dog gets this treat *only* when you are gone.

Step 4: Once your dog can be alone for one hour, you can begin incorporating your departure cues into the exercises. Give your dog his *food Kong* and *treat Kong,* then pick up your keys, purse, briefcase, or other items that your dog sees as an indication that you are leaving. Go to the door and say "See you later," and walk outside. Immediately return, saying a brief "hello," and pick up the *treat Kong.*

Step 5: Repeat step 4, but this time start your car or walk approximately fifty feet from your door before returning.

Step 6: Continue increasing your outside absences in ten-minute intervals until you reach one hour.

Step 7: When your dog can tolerate your absence for one hour, you can begin increasing the interval by an hour each time.

If your dog's separation anxiety is severe or if the above desensitization schedule does not work, you need to call in an expert.

I am grateful to all who made the writing and publication of this book possible:

My brother, Gary; my husband, Kent; and the rest of my wonderful family.

My editor and publisher Julie and everyone at Spiegel & Grau and the Random House family.

My agent, Susan.

The people and dogs of Adopt a Golden Atlanta.

And always the animals, staff, recipients, volunteers, Board of Directors, and donors of Canine Assistants.

I am the luckiest woman on the planet to have all of you in my life. Thank you.

ABOUT THE AUTHOR

PHOTO: © DAVID C. SCOTT

JENNIFER ARNOLD is the founder and executive director of Canine Assistants, a service-dog school based in Milton, Georgia. She is the author of the *New York Times* bestseller *Through a Dog's Eyes,* which was also the subject of a PBS documentary. She lives with her husband, veterinarian Kent Bruner, son Chase, three dogs, Bob the cat, eight horses, and a number of other animals.

Canine Assistants is a nonprofit organization dedicated to providing service dogs for children and adults who have physical disabilities, epilepsy, or other special needs. Canine Assistants does not charge for the service it provides; rather it relies on the generosity of those who recognize that helping one benefits us all.

To learn more about this very special program, please visit their website at www.canineassistants.org or find them on Facebook.